Surviving a Realistic Zombie Apocalypse

Tadhg O'Flaherty

ISBN-13: 978-1-52056-155-4

To the 99%.

Because you deserve to survive.

The elite can only dictate your future if you let them.

Table of Contents

WARNING

The survival techniques described in this book are only to be used during an actual zombie apocalypse, where the safety and future survival of you, your family or friends is at immediate risk. The author does not accept any responsibility for the use or misuse of any material contained in this book. The author is not a certified survival expert or medical doctor and the information contained in this book is not a guarantee of safety or survival.

In some countries, it may be illegal for a citizen to own a firearm or other weapon. Some techniques described may be deemed undesirable by society in general and may also be illegal depending on where you live. Some of these survival techniques may result in injury or death. If you decide to practise any of these survival techniques before a zombie apocalypse then you do so at your own risk. Always consult a competent professional before practising any of the survival or medical techniques described.

This book is intended to be for information purposes only. Some techniques describe in detail how to kill a zombie and should **NOT** be practised before a zombie apocalypse on any living person or animal.

Introduction

"It happened that a fire broke out backstage in a theatre. The clown came out to inform the public. They thought it was jest and applauded. He repeated his warning. They shouted even louder. So I think the world will come to an end amid the general applause from all the wits who believe that it is a joke."
Søren Kierkegaard (1813-1855)

One night you get ready for bed. It's going to be a busy day at the office tomorrow. As you finish getting ready you hear the normal sounds of the city outside your apartment window, some shouting and general sounds of activity. You've heard it all before but as you slowly drift off to sleep those sounds get louder, there is some shooting in the distance when suddenly a blood-curdling scream echoes through the night. It spooks you but you know that you are safe where you are and eventually you drift off into a restless sleep.

The next morning you head out into the city and notice the lack of people around. Maybe it's Sunday so you check your phone to make sure. You see that it is indeed Monday morning but you also notice that your cell phone reception is gone.

On the subway, you notice that the carriage is only about half full than on a normal Monday morning and a lot of people look sick, very sick. When you eventually get to the office you see that most of the team appear to be out sick, strange but not impossible.

You hear some sporadic reports of violent attacks on the news but don't think much of it, it's nearly time to end this strange working day and head home.

While waiting for your train on the underground you notice somebody near you suddenly collapse. Plenty of people rush to help and very soon some medics arrive. As you approach your apartment block you see someone being mugged so you hurry to get indoors.

Things seem a bit strange so you make yourself a cup of coffee and head to the roof where you normally go to unwind while you gaze across the city. This time things are very different. You can see a lot of smoke and fires scattered throughout the city. You hear the sounds of people screaming coming from every direction. You can see a massive group of people running down your street. There are police officers in the crowd who are also running for their lives. There are even police officers on horseback mixed in with the crowd. They all appear to be terrified of something. What are they running from? Every now and then the police turn to fire on an unseen enemy. Someone in the crowd suddenly starts to attack people around them. The police react immediately and gun them down. You have never seen anything like this before.

You try to phone the emergency services to see if you are safe and to find out what is going on but there is no answer. You try to phone friends and family but again there is nobody answering. You run back to your apartment and turn on the TV to see if the local news station is reporting these strange and frightening occurrences but all you get is static. You cycle through all the channels. Some are just static and the rest have a technical difficulties message.

You have absolutely no idea what's going on so you hide behind your window and peek out like a nosey neighbour. Now you can see what's going on more clearly. The people committing the very violent attacks seem to be everywhere. You see a police officer emptying a full magazine of bullets into one of them but he keeps advancing. It's as if the bullets are having no effect whatsoever. The policeman is taken down by this strangely unaffected guy and the attack is so violent and bloody that you can no longer watch. You look away in terror.

It begins to dawn on you what is happening. You have seen this in a thousand zombie movies and TV shows but you can't bring yourself to believe it. The zombie apocalypse has begun. The biggest question that you could ask yourself at this point is *"can I survive this?"*

Are you prepared for what is coming?

How It Can Happen

Before I tell you how it will happen, let me tell you how it will **not** happen. This will not be a virus that can be contracted from bites or exposure to zombies. This will not be an airborne agent that anyone can catch.

It will, however, be an airborne agent that only certain people will contract. This virus will be released as a mist from high altitude aircraft which will continue to spray the entire landmass of Earth for up to 3 days. Over a period of approximately 3 months, certain people will fall victim to the virus. There is absolutely no way of knowing if you are susceptible to contracting the virus as it will be tied to certain DNA sequences. It will affect all walks of life, all races, ages, sexes, etc. and will appear to be completely random yet there is nothing random about those affected. If you have a DNA sequence that is being targeted than you **will** contract the zombie virus.

Even the CDC (Centers for Disease Control and Prevention) in America have posted a preparedness bulletin on their website titled "Preparedness 101: Zombie Apocalypse" that outlines the supplies needed in the event of such a disaster. Such American organisations are notorious for not having a sense of humour. They are taking the threat seriously and so should you.

Modern cases

On 26th May 2012 Rudy Eugene attacked homeless man Ronald Poppo on the MacArthur Causeway in Miami Florida. This wasn't any type of ordinary attack. Eugene literally ate Poppo's face and consumed the flesh. A Miami police officer initially responded to the incident and shot Eugene once before ultimately killing him. That first bullet had no effect whatsoever on Eugene and he continued his violent attack without missing a beat.

News reports at the time claimed the Eugene was high on the drug bath salts, however, no matter what kind of drug you have taken, you will react when someone shoots you. You will feel pain or acknowledge the damage done to you.

Eugene was shot and simply carried on eating without any indication that he had been injured. According to witnesses police fired up to 6 shots during the incident. Controversy was raised at the time when the toxicologist was unable to confirm whether or not Eugene had traces of bath salts in his system.

Eugene's girlfriend, in an interview with CBS news, stated that, although he smoked marijuana, he had never taken any stronger recreational drugs and refused to take general medications for basic ailments such as headaches.

Despite the massive use of bath salts throughout the world, there have only been a handful of zombie cases contributed to the drug. Two zombie cases alone occurred in Miami coinciding with the Eugene case.

There are 8 privately owned biological laboratories in Miami alone. Eglin Air Force Base in Valparaiso, Florida has been used for biological weapons tests in the past. I am not accusing any private company or military installation of complicity in previous or future zombie infections.

Another strange new zombie case has erupted in Uganda with up to 3,000 children affected by a condition known as Nodding Disease which has all the hallmarks of a zombie virus. Affected children are left in a condition of being physically stunned and severely mentally disabled. These children have been known to wander off and have also been known to growl and shuffle around in a strange manner. They have been unofficially dubbed *"zombie children"*. There is no known cure for this condition and the WHO (World Health Organisation) remains baffled by its sudden appearance.

All of these are just test cases, experiments in order to judge public opinion and to iron out the final wrinkles in the viral agent.

Laws, Government and the Military

Before the zombie apocalypse takes hold it is imperative that you live within the laws of your country. The reason for this is because if you are incarcerated in prison when disaster strikes **you will not survive**. Do not get in trouble with the law, pay your taxes, drive within the speed limit and do not draw any unwanted attention to yourself. If you are currently serving probation it is even more important for you to not only obey the law but also distance yourself from any individuals that are not law abiding citizens, as hanging around with these people could land you in trouble again.

The one world government will collapse shortly after the beginning of the zombie apocalypse and all control will pass to small regional political systems. Before the full collapse of the government, they will enact laws that will enable them to carry out their ultimate plan. Due to these laws, the military in your country will begin sweeping through towns and cities. It will ultimately take many years for the one world government to regain some semblance of their previous power.

The first time the military comes to your city it will appear that their intention is to kill zombies when, in reality, they will be there to take out specific targets, whether they are zombie or human. The second time they visit your city it will be to round you up in order to transport you to a safe, secure facility where you will be protected. Nothing could be further from the truth. **Do not go with them**.

If you live in America do not go anywhere near a FEMA camp. They are specifically designed to keep you contained within the fences. Besides, it took FEMA 5 days to get water to the Superdome following hurricane Katrina that struck New Orleans in 2005. FEMA will be used in collaboration with the military to move groups of survivors to massive camps. You do not want to be in one of these during the zombie apocalypse.

Laws

Small regional authorities will enact sweeping changes to laws that govern criminal activity such as looting. There will no longer be any place where they can house prisoners so most crimes will only have one punishment, the death penalty. Police and soldiers will be tasked with not only preventing crime but also with carrying out executions. All conventional laws and courts will be suspended in favour of military tribunal. Do not expect any sympathy being granted to you if you are brought before one of these tribunals. There will be no version of death row and those sentenced to death will be killed within minutes or hours of their sentence being handed down.

Avoiding the military

Before the apocalypse, you may decide to stock-up on supplies, however, if you use a credit card or even a loyalty card in a shop the government will immediately know what you have bought and how much of each item you have purchased. Pay for items with cash only. Militaries and governments across the world have lists of individuals who are stockpiling and they will come for your supplies when they feel the time is right. Several TV shows have appeared recently that depict preppers. It shows what they are planning and the supplies they have stockpiled. By appearing on TV, these people have managed to paint a target on their supplies for not only the military but also, people in their neighbourhood will know that they have food and will come to loot it. Do not risk your supplies being confiscated, they are your supplies and should be protected.

If you live in a city or small town at the beginning of the apocalypse you will need to get out ASAP. Don't wait around to see if you will be rescued as you will not be. It could take up to 6 months for the military to complete their sweeps. Get out of the city and if you want to return you will need to watch carefully from a safe distance and only return once you are certain that they will not be coming back. I do not advise returning to any city or built-up urban area as these places will be far too dangerous for anyone to survive effectively. Try your best to find an isolated house in the countryside that is as far away from built-up areas as possible.

Looting

Almost all products in all urban and built-up areas around the entire world will be looted within the first 3 days. Looting will be an extremely dangerous undertaking during this time and should be avoided if possible. If you don't have any supplies gathered than you will need to go looting but be advised that you may not survive. You will find yourself up against very desperate humans who have not prepared along with zombies trying to eat you. Police and military personnel will be out in force and they will shoot you on sight. It doesn't matter if you have only looted water or formula to feed your child, you will be shot on sight.

If you do encounter the police or military while you are looting, drop your supplies immediately and run away as fast as you can. Don't try to plead with them or appeal to their better side. They are just as much afraid and trigger happy as anyone else during these dark and desperate times.

Currency and Trade

Many preppers stock up on silver and gold bullion but during a zombie apocalypse, these items will become absolutely worthless, in saying that you may have some success with bullion, cash and credit cards in the first 3 days. Be warned that within this time there will be severe runs on banks and ATM machines. Police and military forces will be deployed to banks and ATM machines in an attempt to keep some semblance of order and people will be killed in these areas.

On day one make every effort to get to an ATM machine and draw the maximum allowable on any bank cards and credit cards that you have. Spend this money as soon as possible on tangible items like water and food.

Trade any bullion or high-value electronic devices such as smartphones, laptops, tablets, etc. for water and food. Any luxury items such as artwork or decorative items in your house should also be traded for water and food if possible.

In the future, the most valuable trading currencies will be clean fresh water, food and toilet paper. Everybody needs water and food to survive and if you have these commodities in abundance you can trade these for tools or other survival equipment. Toilet paper will be a luxury item in the future because it will never be produced ever again.

When trading with others it is vital that you do not let them know that you have stocks of supplies, they must not be allowed to know where you live and always take extreme care as people will be more than willing to kill in order to get supplies for themselves. If you decide to approach a group in order to establish trade links do not enter their compound or house. Stay outside and try to get one of them to meet you in order to discuss terms. If a group approaches your compound or house a similar tactic must be employed. Once they leave your house stay on high alert for several weeks because they may come back as a group to raid your supplies.

Basic Essentials

During the zombie apocalypse, you need to be prepared to move at very short notice. Your shelter could be compromised and you may be facing multiple zombies so being prepared to run is vital. But what do you take with you? Have a quick look around your home right now. What would you take with you if disaster was to strike with only 2 minutes notice? You might take a bottle or two of water, maybe a knife from the kitchen, maybe some sentimental items off the shelf and jump into your car to make your escape. But what if your car wouldn't start or you don't own a car? Maybe you live in the centre of London or Manhattan and have always relied on the underground rail network. Now you have to move on foot, avoiding zombies and itchy trigger finger humans with only two bottles of water, a knife, some keepsakes and the clothes on your back. You may end up being on the run for the rest of your life. Those two bottles of water will be gone very soon and it will get cold during the night. What clothes are you wearing? Are these good enough for cold nights outside?

Having a pack prepared is essential to surviving while on the run. Many preppers will keep ready packed supplies close to the front door or in their car called a *"bug-out-bag"*. But what supplies need to be packed in order to not only survive but still be able to move with a lot of supplies over your shoulder? The most important aspect of a bug-out-bag is to only take the essentials needed for survival. It is a waste of space and ineffective to pack your wedding album or your kids drawings that are normally pinned to the fridge. Never feel guilty about leaving these sentimental things behind as they are not crucial to your survival.

Backpack
You will need a sturdy, yet comfortable backpack to carry all of these supplies. It will most likely need to be very large. Always avoid gear bags or anything that requires you to carry it in your hand as this will have to be dropped any time you need to confront a zombie or aggressive human. The

backpack should be bought after you have gathered the supplies listed below because only then will you know the size you need.

Watch and compass
- Wrist watch
- Compass

The watch should be a wind-up version as you can no longer rely on batteries. Get into the habit of winding this watch every day. Just before you bug out check that the correct time is set on this watch as you may not get a chance to do so later. Make sure the compass is of a high quality and works correctly.

Torch and batteries
- Large torch
- Small torch
- Headlamp
- Wind-up torch
- Batteries AAA x40
- Batteries AA x40
- Anglers' glow sticks x50

Pack at least two battery operated torches plus a headlamp. Carry as many batteries as possible as well as some rechargeable batteries and a solar charging kit. Do not use the rechargeable batteries until the regular ones have been exhausted first. Conserve battery usage as much as possible while on the run. Bring a wind-up torch also but don't rely exclusively on this as you may need a torch at a time when silence is necessary, however, the wind-up torch will be very loud when charging. You do not need very large glow sticks. Small sized fishing style glow sticks can still provide enough light and usually come in packs of 50 and can provide a steady stream of light for up to 10 hours.

Food and water
- Drinking water x3 litres
- Water purification tablets x10
- Water filter
- Condoms x10
- Energy bars x10
- Tinned food x5
- MREs x20

- Collapsible water bottle
- Small fishing kit
- Snare wire

Water is the most important thing to pack as the human body can only survive without water for about 3 days. In contrast, you can survive for about 3 weeks without food. The minimum amount of water you need is 3 litres (6 pints). After this bring as much as you can physically carry. Water purification tablets and a filter system are also recommended in the event that you gather water while on the run. Condoms can hold up to 2 litres (4.2 pints) of water. Bring enough food to last for a minimum of 3 days. Have as much variety in your food as possible; don't rely on a single type of food. Split this between energy bars, tinned foods and MREs (meals ready to eat) which can be purchased from military supply stores. The collapsible water bottle should be carried empty and can be used when you settle down for the night and have a ready supply of water nearby. These collapsible water bottles can hold up to 20 litres (42.3 pints). By having a compact fishing kit and snare wire you have the opportunity of catching fresh food while on the run.

Maps and guides
- Local ordinance survey map
- Compact survival guide
- Compact first aid book
- Zip-lock plastic bags x10
- Shrink wrap x2

Make sure that you include maps of your local area. There is no need to keep detailed maps of your entire country or even maps of other countries as the chances are that you will not be able to travel very far after you go on the run. A vital component of your bug-out-bag will be a compact first aid reference manual. If you get injured you will most likely be on your own. Do not expect help from anyone. Carry a compact survival guide as these often contain vital life-saving skills and techniques that you can reference while on the move. Ensure that all books and paper are adequately wrapped in plastic to ensure they don't get destroyed if you need to wade through a river. Do not rely solely on your own printouts of various survival tips as this paper will be of a low quality in comparison to books and will not hold up to rough treatment for very long.

Tools
- Survival knife
- Multi-tool
- Entrenching tool
- Small axe
- Duct tape x3 rolls
- Machete
- Butane lighters x5
- Matches x10 packs
- Permanent match lighter
- Flint lighter
- Lighter fluid x3
- Magnifying glass

You might be tempted to take a lot of specialised tools that do plenty of individual jobs but you must also remain conscious of the amount of things you are carrying with you. If you take everything in the tool shed with you then how do you expect to outrun a bunch of fast moving zombies? Only take those tools that are essential to survival.

An entrenching tool can be used to dig a latrine or foxhole and folds up making it an ideal alternative to a full sized shovel. Multiple lighting sources are necessary. Butane lighters will eventually run out of gas. Once these are exhausted use your matches. Be sure to wrap the boxes of matches in shrink wrap and keep these in a zip-lock bag to keep them dry. A permanent match lighter could be good for up to 15,000 strikes per fill of lighter fluid. The last resort is a flint lighter which only produces a spark.

Ensure that the container of lighter fluid is kept as far away from all ignition sources as one spark could set your bug-out-bag on fire or even explode causing injury. In a pinch, you can use a magnifying glass to start a fire if it is a sunny day.

First aid

Carry a small first aid kit ensuring that you take extra scissors and bandages. While on the run always be on the lookout for extra medical supplies as you don't know how long you will be moving for or what levels of injuries you may encounter along the way. If you run out of bandages you can make new ones by cutting up T-shirts. This could bring an added level of danger as you may need to enter shopping centres or other zombie-riddled areas to find new, unused T-shirts.

Bring a small bottle of red wine as part of your medical supplies as this can help to reduce the rate of radiation absorption from fallout after a nuclear explosion. Drink the wine approximately 30 minutes after the nuclear blast, as this is the time that fallout is returning to Earth from the upper atmosphere. This is not a cure-all but will slow down the rate at which radioactive fallout affects the Thyroid gland.

Cooking

- Can opener (P-38)
- Camping stove
- Cooking pot
- Eating utensils

The P-38 is a tiny and lightweight military style can opener that was first developed in 1942 and was issued to military personnel. When choosing a camping stove, do not rely on one that requires a separate gas canister as this adds to the weight in your bug-out-bag. Instead, choose one that allows you to add your own lighting materials. Eating utensils and a cooking pot can be purchased from any good hiking store.

Clothing

The clothes you pack will depend on the part of the world you are in and the climate conditions you are likely to face. Clothes should be layered to maintain internal body temperature. It is important to bring at least two sets of clothes so you can change if one set is wet. You must minimise the possibility of getting sick of suffering from hypothermia as much as possible.

Pack plenty of fresh socks as you will need to change these often to help prevent trench rot, which was prevalent during the trench warfare of World War One. Ensure that you pack comfortable, broken-in hiking boots. Extra sets of shoelaces are a must, not only as replacements for your boots but they can also be used for various things that require tying objects together.

Mental health
- Journal
- Several pens and pencils
- Non-fragrant soap
- Deck of playing cards
- Small towel
- Travel size toothbrush
- Toothpaste

It is vital to keep your spirits up when on the run. Bring a journal that includes a calendar so you can keep detailed notes about any potential food or water sources that you come across and tick off the days. It is very important to keep track of what day it is, but only for the reason of keeping your mental health in check. Personal hygiene is necessary for keeping your spirits high. You should wash whenever it is safe to do so. If possible wash your clothes.

Shelter

You're going to need to bed down for the night and can't rely on finding an abandoned house along the way so bring a tent and sleeping bag. It could get very cold at night so pack a warm woollen blanket. A large tarp is also necessary in case you lose your tent or need to extend your tent to provide cover while you dry clothes or cook. A ground mat, similar to a yoga mat will provide some support while you sleep. This is vital because if you wake each morning with bed pains and muscle tension you will not be able to function at your best while on the run.

Other supplies
- Wind-up AM/FM radio
- Mobile phone
- Wind-up charger

- Solar charger
- Gas mask
- Compact binoculars
- Paracord x15 metres (50 feet)
- Safety goggles
- Sunglasses
- Work gloves
- Rain poncho
- Toilet paper
- Candles x5

Communication could prove to be vital for your survival while on the run. The mobile phone that you bring should be an old, yet working model as these keep their charge for a long time, unlike smartphones. Even though most, if not all, modern infrastructure will fail shortly after a zombie apocalypse begins, the mobile network may still function for a short period of time. Contact with family and friends can give you vital information about the current state of the world.

A gas mask is necessary if you encounter tear gas or other undesirable airborne particles. Candles will be your last option should you run out of other sources of light but should be considered to be as dangerous as smoking in bed. Be very careful or you could not only lose your tent but potentially burn to death if these candles are not extinguished properly.

Only select a suitable backpack once you have gathered all the items above so you have a good idea of the size needed. When packing your bug-out-bag be aware that realistic zombies will not be the clumsy, slow moving, moronic types that are depicted in various movies and TV shows. They will be intelligent and will be on the lookout for their next victim. With this in mind, it is important to ensure that you pack everything in such a way that nothing will rattle and there will be no noise whatsoever coming from you or your backpack. It is also equally important to ensure that nothing shiny will reflect light. These two things will quickly give away your position but can be easily dealt with by a generous application of black tape to anything that rattles or shines.

Items that you do not need until after you set up your tent, such as the paracord should be packed at the very bottom of the backpack while items you will need in a hurry should be packed at the top or in external pockets. Some items can be tied to the outside of your backpack rather than being packed, thus saving some space for other things.

Always be prepared to go on the run. Spend your free time walking various different routes from your home and taking notes of any good camping areas, streams, or any area that might provide cover should you need to hide. Do as much research as possible. Where are you ultimately going to go when you need to run from your home? Have you selected one specific location? What if that location is compromised, where will you go then? Formulate multiple escape routes from your home and keep notes in your journal about all possible safe zones along your route. It is vital that you have multiple final destinations in case the main one should become unavailable.

If there are multiple people in your party you will need an identical bug-out-bag for each person with the exception that you will need to add several two-way radios and extra batteries for these. Each member should carry their own radio and only turn these on once someone becomes separated from your group in order to save power. Smaller bug-out-bags will need to be prepared for children as they may not be able to carry everything on the list above.

Water

During a zombie apocalypse water will be your first priority. Humans can only survive for about 3 days without water. While on the run take note of any potential water sources in your journal so that you can return to these at a later stage. The average person needs to consume around 2 litres (4.2 pints) of water each day. We lose water through physical exertion, fever, smoking, vomiting, diarrhoea and even while eating food.

Dehydration

When we lose too much water from our system we will become dehydrated. The symptoms of dehydration include:

- Increased thirst
- Weakness
- Dizziness
- Sluggishness
- Confusion
- Fainting
- Being unable to sweat

- Decreased urine output
- Swollen tongue

When suffering from dehydration it is vital that you must increase your water intake immediately. If you don't seek out fresh water you will begin to experience extreme confusion followed by headaches and seizures. Eventually, you will suffer from difficulty in breathing, chest pains and fainting followed by lapsing into a coma and ultimately dying.

Rationing

If you are running low on water or are hiding from zombies and don't know when you will be able to move again you will need to maximise the limited water at your disposal. Only drink when you are desperately thirsty but don't guzzle down loads of your limited supply. Instead, use enough water to basically wet your lips and then hold out for as long as possible before doing this again. The following techniques will help in retaining fluids when water is scarce.

- If you are a smoker, stop until you can replenish your water supply
- Stay in the shade and avoid exposure to the sun
- Avoid eating food as this will use valuable fluids
- Do not drink alcohol as this will make you even more dehydrated
- Avoid physical exertion

Assuming that you are not on the run and have established a permanent or semi-permanent place to stay you will need to source water immediately. This is your first priority. If you are in a building you may be thinking that there is no need to worry because the tap is running perfectly so there will be an unlimited supply of water. This water supply will not last because eventually, all electricity will stop working, including the power that is supplied to pumps that push that water supply to your faucet. If you are lucky enough to find a working tap take full advantage of this immediately by filling as many containers as possible with water. If there is a bath in the house fill this with water.

If you have decided to stay in a city or town there may be a shopping centre nearby. This has the potential to be a treasure trove of supplies, including bottled water, provided it has not been badly looted. But venturing out to raid this shopping centre presents extreme danger from attack by, not only zombies but also other desperate humans who are willing to kill to get supplies.

You will still need to find a permanent source of drinking water if you are to survive in this apocalyptic future world. If you are lucky there will be a stream or river nearby. Even if the water looks clear and fresh it will need to be filtered and purified before drinking. The easiest way to purify water is to boil it.

When drinking any new source of water it is best to test it first. Rub some of the water on your arm and wait 12 hours. If there are any blotches or redness on your arm do not drink this water. After this wet your lips and wait another 12 hours. If there are no problems drink a small amount of water and wait another 12 hours. If after this time you do not suffer from any stomach cramps or nausea then the water is safe to drink. To sterilise drinking water before use add 2 drops of bleach to every litre (2.1 pints).

If you come across a static pool of water where there is no vegetation growing around it then it is more than likely polluted and should be avoided at all costs. Never drink sea water, no matter how tempted you might be, as this will kill you. If you are in extremely cold conditions do not eat snow to get water as this will lower your internal temperature and you could easily die from hypothermia. Boil snow before drinking it.

Set up water butts on the rain gutters around your house to gather as much rainwater as possible. Ensure that all gutters are cleaned regularly. There will be nothing wrong with rain water unless a nuclear bomb has exploded nearby. Take full advantage of any rainfall by placing clean empty buckets and containers around your garden. If you are lucky enough to have a pick-up truck you could search in nearby hardware stores for gigantic water containers such as specifically designed plastic water tanks or even new plastic oil containers can work.

Set this up on the ground floor of your house and pour any collected rainwater into this container for use later. Avoid keeping things you will need outside your house as you will need to go outside, into potential danger to get these things when you need them.

Water should always be stored in a cool dark place. Never allow any containers of water to sit in direct sunlight as this will encourage the growth of green algae. Do not become complacent with your water supply as this can run out very quickly. If you can come across a large continuous supply of water try to create a makeshift shower system. This is very important for keeping your spirits up during a crisis. Collect the water from this shower, filter it and reuse it for future showers. Do not use the discarded shower water for drinking.

Food

After water, food is the second biggest priority during a realistic zombie apocalypse. If you stay in your house during the initial phases of the apocalypse then you may still have electrical power for a few days. Perishable items, fruits and vegetables, as well as items from the fridge or freezer should be eaten first. Do not rely on your fridge or freezer to stay operational. Always expect your electricity to turn off at any minute. The only exception to this is if you have a solar or wind power system that is reliable.

Calories

Calories are the body's fuel. Food is turned into energy and this energy is calculated in units of calories. The average adult will need to consume approximately 2,500 calories per day. This measurement is based on an average adult during peace times when they are going about a normal average day; however, during the zombie apocalypse, you will be doing far more physical work so your calorie use will probably jump to over 3,500 calories. This large amount of energy will require a larger amount of food, being consumed, than you are used to.

Vitamins

The food you consume will contain small amounts of vitamins that are vital for staying healthy. Vitamin C works fantastically at boosting the immune system. If during the early days of the zombie apocalypse, you are able to do a big looting of a shopping centre I would suggest that you take as much orange juice and vitamin C tablets as you can. Minor illness can put you out of action to such an extent that you will no longer be able to fight effectively. When you are sick you will require larger amounts of fresh water but you may not have the ability or energy to gather further water supplies. Avoiding illness will become vital during the apocalypse.

Another important vitamin for humans is vitamin D. This can be produced in your system by simply exposing yourself to sunlight. It may not be the best idea to go outside during the daytime but if you are able, you should take full advantage of this.

The most important vitamins and what foods contain them are:

- Vitamin A (carrots)
- B Vitamins (grains, potatoes, bananas, beans)
- Vitamin C (oranges, kiwi, grapefruits, strawberries)
- Vitamin D (sunlight, eggs, fish)
- Vitamin E (almonds, sunflower seeds, tomatoes)
- Vitamin K (spinach, Brussel sprouts, broccoli)
- Folic Acid (citrus fruits, peas, lentils, cauliflower)
- Calcium (yoghurt, cheese, milk)
- Iron (liver, soybeans, spinach)
- Zinc (cashews, dark chocolate, beans)

Animals

If you have no other food source available and don't have any prospect of finding food anytime soon you can eat your family pet. Dogs and cats can provide a sizable enough meal when faced with an emergency. I know pets can quickly become a valued member of any family but may have to be sacrificed in favour of your survival.

When preparing an animal for consumption it is important to remove all skin and internal organs before cooking.

Birds will need to have their feathers plucked and you will need to drain all blood from their system before cooking.

The following is a list of some animals that can be safely eaten:
- Cattle
- Sheep
- Goats
- Bears
- Foxes
- Deer
- Rabbits
- Pigs

- Guinea pigs
- Squirrels
- Lizards
- Turtles
- Raccoons
- Snakes
- Birds

Avoid eating rats as these are notorious for carrying disease. Ensure that all meat is cooked thoroughly as stomach upsets will become a major hindrance during the zombie apocalypse.

If at all possible, gather domestic animals such as cattle, sheep, pigs and chickens and bring them back to your home. But be warned, these animals will create noise that can, and probably will attract zombies. It would be better to house these animals in an area that is a minimum of 1km (0.6 miles) away from your house to afford you with some semblance of security. You will need to travel to this location every day in order to care for the animals which will present a further risk.

If you are preparing a rabbit and it shows any signs of myxomatosis discard this kill immediately and sterilise your hands, hunting tools or implements that may have come into contact with this animal. Do not hunt for any more rabbits in the area where you caught this infected one. Myxomatosis is a disease that affects rabbits and causes them to suffer a gruesome death.

Hunting

Hunting with a rifle used to be perfectly acceptable, however there now exists the danger that a zombie or human will be alerted by gunfire. Where possible use silent weapons such as bow and arrow, crossbow, knife or animal traps.

You will need great patience when it comes to trapping animals as they are generally cunning and will avoid unusual-looking objects. Carefully observe the animals that you intend to trap to see where they usually graze or if there are any specific trails that they regularly use for crossing from one area to another.

Do not waste any time trying to hunt animals in their lair as these have been carefully selected and reinforced to stop other creatures being able to snatch them. This frustrating hunt will only result in you expelling more energy and going home empty handed.

Make it a habit to collect any arrows that you fire during hunting as you don't know when you will run out or when you may encounter a hunting goods store in order to replenish your supply. Most arrows are produced for sport and are designed to be shot at soft targets. Any arrows you gather should be reinforced by wrapping them in black tape. The tape should be very tightly wound in order to maintain aerodynamic traits and should also cover the base of the arrowhead. This has the added bonus of stopping any glare from the metal shaft.

If you are well practised you can use a slingshot for hunting. The best type of ammo to use in this scenario is small metal ball-bearings. The smooth surface of the ball-bearing ensures a steady enough flight from the projectile while the weight could help with killing an animal. For large land-based animals, it is best to aim for the head as you will probably not get enough force to penetrate the skin. If you can hit the animal in the correct part of the head you may stun it or render it unconscious. If you are successful get to the animal quickly and kill it, before it has a chance to recover and potentially retaliate.

The easiest trap that you could construct would be a loop of wire that you tie to a tree. The end tied to the tree should be very secure with a loose loop at the other end. Use some small sticks to support the loop about 7.5cm (3 inches) off the ground. An animal will walk into this loop and immediately panic. During this state of panic, the loop will close around the animals head or a limb and get tighter as the animal struggles. The reason for keeping the loop so close to the ground is that this can trap small, as well as, large animals. You can always create more elaborate traps if you like but there is no need, besides there may never be an animal caught by this elaborate trap because they simply don't come across it. This could easily prove to be a waste of time and energy.

Fishing

Another easy way to hunt food is to use a large net in a nearby stream to catch fish. Ensure that the net is properly secured to both sides of the bank and check it regularly. If you trap too many things in the net it could easily fail and leave you without this valuable method of hunting food.

If you don't have a large net you can use a basic fishing rod to catch fish. Having multiple hooks on the line can increase your chances of catching multiple fish. The most basic food to use in order to lure a fish to bite the hook is earthworms. You can either dig for these or pour a slightly soapy solution onto bare earth and wait for the worms to emerge.

Clean plastic bottles can be used for trapping small fish. Unscrew the cap and secure some bait in the bottom of the bottle. Place the bottle in a stream in such a way as the open side is facing into the current. Place some stones or sand in the bottle to hold it in place on the river bed. If you have any string you can tie this around the top of the bottle and secure this to a nearby branch so you don't lose your trap. Small fish will swim into the bottle to retrieve the bait but will not be able to swim back out the open top section.

If you come across any body of water that has dead fish either on the surface or washed up on the edges it is vital that you abandon this area as a possible fishing spot because it is highly likely that this water is contaminated and the resulting fish will either make you sick or could kill you if eaten.

When preparing fish remove all scales with a knife, cut open the fish's belly and remove all internal organs. Just like birds, fish should be drained of all blood before cooking. Remove the head, tail, fins and gills.

Preserving food

Fresh meats such as cuts of beef or fish can be preserved by drying them out or smoking them. You do not need a freezer to keep meat in an edible state. To dry out meat simply rub it in salt, if available, and hang this in a cool dry area of your house. If you decide to smoke your meats, be aware that the smoke can easily draw the attention of zombies or other humans and thus give away your position. It is best practice to always think strategically when performing any action that could easily give away your position.

A more permanent solution is to have enough solar or wind energy gathering devices available to provide power to a freezer. Before freezing the meat you will need to wrap it in plastic to stop the freezing from doing damage to the structure of the meat. If there is a butcher shop near your house it might be advantageous to raid the place for vacuum packing equipment. This may also prove to be a valuable source of knives and other potential weapons. You never know, they might still have electrical power and their freezers could be filled with meat.

One of the greatest food stores you could get your hands on is dried rice. As long as you keep this dry and vacuum sealed it could last indefinitely. Technically you can survive on rice as your only food source if needed. Many countries in Asia use rice as their main food source without any major ill effects.

The following is a list of foods that can last forever if stored correctly:
- Honey
- Rice
- Sugar
- Maple syrup
- Vanilla extract
- Distilled white vinegar
- Salt
- Corn-starch

Salt

Salt is not only useful as a preservative but is also vital for human existence. You may find that you are not getting enough foods with an appropriate level of salt to prolong your existence. If that is the case you will need to add just a pinch of salt to half a litre (1 pint) of water. Do not take the salt neat, only take it when it is diluted in water and don't exceed a single pinch or you could find yourself in big trouble.

The biggest indicators of possible salt deficiency are nausea and muscle cramps. These could, of course, be symptoms of something else but you won't know until after you have tried to replace missing salt in your system. Do not repeat the above process until you have waited for at least 24-hours.

Food is all around you. All you have to do is search for it. One of the biggest foodstuffs to stay away from is mushrooms as some of these can be extremely poisonous and could kill you.

In the long run, you will need to establish a more permanent source of food. As corner stores and shopping centres will never exist again you will need to gather vegetable and fruit seeds as well as livestock and become a farmer.

Zombie Killing Myths

You are used to seeing zombies in movies and on TV shows as bumbling brain-dead simpletons that slowly shuffle about, are easy to avoid and are useless with everyday things like opening doors. These zombie depictions can only be killed by destroying the brain. Some shows will display severed zombie heads that are still animated and can bite you if you get too close.

The zombies that you will face will be nothing like these fictional depictions. They will be flesh and blood human beings that can be killed just as easily as any other human being. The big difference between a normal human and a zombie is that the zombie will have extremely heightened adrenalin and will not feel any pain. These rage filled creatures will maintain any attack until they are killed.

When you fire at a normal human they will instinctively duck for cover. They will have a high fear level associated with being injured. If you shoot a human being in the shoulder they will probably drop to the ground in agony and will shuffle away behind some cover. Fear can easily cause a human to flee a firefight. But this will not be the case with a zombie.

If you shoot a zombie in the shoulder they will appear completely unaffected and will continue to advance on you. These zombies will move fast, very fast. All they want to do is kill you by any means at their disposal. It is your duty to react quickly and drop that zombie.

As with human beings, the only way to ensure a kill is to take out as many vital organs as possible, such as brain, heart, lungs, etc. Shoot a zombie in the heart and you will kill it instantly. If you find yourself pinned down by a zombie in hand-to-hand combat and can't draw your weapon effectively try your best to stab at vital organs or sever a major artery. When mortally wounded, a zombie will die just as quickly as a human being.

Wherever possible, take out a zombie from a distance and then turn and run as far as you can. The zombie may not be alone. Your best chance of survival is to run and evade.

Weapons

During the zombie apocalypse weapons will be absolutely vital if you are to survive for any length of time. Not only will killing zombies become part and parcel of daily life but you may also need to defend yourself against other human beings who want to take your supplies or gangs of humans who get their kicks out of hunting down and killing people. Any serial killers who have survived the initial days of the apocalypse will be in their element as there will be no more police forces tracking them down.

Guns

If you live in America you will have easy access to guns and ammunition. If however, you live in Ireland or England it will be a lot more difficult to arm yourself once a zombie apocalypse takes hold. Take some time to identify your nearest gun shop as you may need to raid this store on the first or second day of the initial zombie outbreak.

Are any of your neighbour's avid hunters or own guns for defence? They may have abandoned their home at the start of the zombie outbreak and maybe, just maybe they have left their guns behind.

The best combination of guns to have at your disposal is:

- Hunting rifle
- Shotgun
- Assault rifle
- Handgun

The guns you select should be basic, easy to strip down, easy to clean and easy to re-assemble. The most reliable gun in the world is the Russian-made Kalashnikov AK-47. If you are faced with looting a gun shop this **must** be the first weapon you should take. The AK-47 can be buried in a pool of mud and will fire as soon as you take it out of the mud. No other weapon in the world is capable of this. The AK-47 contains only 8 moving parts and can be stripped down in less than 1 minute. It is very easy to clean and maintain.

During the Vietnam war, it was common for US soldiers to abandon their M16 assault rifles in favour of AK-47's taken from fallen enemy soldiers.

The biggest question you may face is ... how much ammo should I have? The easiest answer is to take as much ammo as you can, as often as you can.

When going up against a zombie you will find yourself firing a large amount of ammo. The common perception, from movies and TV shows, is that you will take out a zombie with a single shot. This is simply not true. When being attacked, you will be completely struck with fear, adrenaline will be pumping through your system at a high level and your aim **will** be off. Never aim for a headshot as the head is a very small target and you will miss most of the time. Instead, you should aim for the torso (stomach and chest). Not only does this area provide a much bigger target but it will also contain almost all of the major organs.

You might think that it would be better to have as much military weaponry and hardware as possible in order to increase your chances of survival, and you would be right, but do not, under any circumstances, approach a military base during or after the zombie apocalypse as you stand almost no chance of survival. Even if a military base appears abandoned it is most likely fully occupied with soldiers who are taking cover.

Some military style weapons and handguns may be available in police stations, even in countries where guns are not generally available, such as Ireland or England. The only problem with this is that the police officers will most likely take all the weapons with them when they either abandon the station or lock it down in an attempt to defend the building. As with military bases, you may not survive a trip to a police station.

Bow and arrow

If you can get your hands on a good quality archery set this can prove to be an effective weapon, not only for hunting but also for killing zombies. You will need to practice with this on a daily basis in order to perfect your aim and the speed that you can reload. Hunting and sporting stores will almost always stock bow and arrows.

The best kind of archery bow to use during a zombie apocalypse is a compound bow. These will be easily identifiable by their intricate system of pulleys and cables. These types of bows will give you plenty of time to aim while you have the cable fully drawn back without causing muscle fatigue. The biggest drawback with these bows is that you will need a good deal of strength in order to initially draw back the cable. Compound bows are usually made from metal or carbon fibre and are a lot less affected by changes in climate.

You will need to gather as many arrows, as often as possible, and reclaim any used arrows whenever possible. If you come across a container of arrowheads but no actual arrows, take these as you can fashion arrows in the future or you may come across a collection of arrows at a later stage that do not have any arrowheads on them.

Try to get an over-the-shoulder quiver for holding your arrows. Some bows and crossbows will be able to accommodate a few arrows but you will need to carry as many arrows as possible. When training with a bow take advantage of your quiver and perfect your method of drawing an arrow from the quiver, loading it in the bow, drawing back the cable, aiming and firing on your target. The faster you can do this process the more arrows you will be able to successfully launch at your target.

If you can find a compound crossbow take this also. The compound crossbow may be able to accept standard arrows also, depending on the type you get.

Spear

Hunting and sporting stores may also have javelins. These can make a very effective spear and do not need to be exclusively thrown at your target. Remember that any weapon you throw may be lost forever. If you throw a spear, ninja star, or throwing knives you may still need to evacuate the area if more enemies approach. In this scenario it will, more than likely, result in your death if you attempt to retrieve these weapons.

You won't need more than 2 or 3 javelins and these can't be considered a primary weapon. These should only be used as a last resort weapon because you will either be throwing it away or using it up close. If you are being attacked by multiple enemies you cannot afford to throw this weapon and should consider it a close quarters, hand-to-hand weapon.

Slingshot

A slingshot will not be the most effective weapon during a zombie apocalypse. The only reason I mention it here is that in most countries around the world it may prove difficult to start off with a gun or other lethal weapon. The only reason to use a slingshot would be as a distraction weapon. In order to draw attention away from yourself, you could fire at steel garage doors or windows. If you are up against armed humans and are able to distract them enough you may be able to infiltrate their camp and steal some weapons. In this scenario, it is vital to leave the area as soon as you have acquired a weapon and put a sizable distance between you and your enemy.

Knives

Knives will probably be the first weapon you will have at your disposal during the zombie apocalypse as these are everywhere you look. There are knives in your kitchen, in your shed or you may have a sword on display in your house. Your knife is so vital to your survival that it is paramount to ensure that any knives you have are sharpened at all times. If you do not have a knife sharpener at home you can easily find these in hardware stores. Ensure that sharpening stones are kept lubricated while sharpening the knife to prevent damage. Using basic household oil is perfect for this job.

Any knife you carry should always be kept in a suitable sheath to minimise the risk of cutting yourself. Even a small cut can easily become infected and lead to sepsis (blood poisoning) and will become very difficult to impossible for you to treat successfully.

Knives will only be an effective weapon during close-range hand-to-hand combat. When going up against a zombie remember that they will not feel any pain. Stabbing them repeatedly may have no effect unless you are able to hit vital organs. When faced with a zombie attack it is best to stab at the brain, heart or lungs. Once the zombie drops it is best to run rather than staying and finishing the job. If you have done enough damage the zombie will not survive for very long anyway.

Defences

Defences are absolutely necessary if you are going to survive for any length of time during the zombie apocalypse.

Walls

Walls can be very effective in keeping out zombies if they are built with defence in mind. There is no need to build a 30 metre (100 feet) high wall. Some of the best defensive walls can be seen at prisons and you should build walls based on the prison system. These walls have a rounded top section that is covered in grease making them impossible to grab onto. The highest wall you will need is 3 metres (10 feet) high. If you don't have walls around your house you will need to raid a hardware or building supply store for concrete blocks, cement, sand, gravel, plastic piping, axle grease and tools. Wherever possible attempt to estimate the amount of supplies you will need and take a further 10% just to be sure. You do not want to take too many trips to get supplies as each trip will increase your chances of an attack.

To build a defensive wall you will first need to dig out a square ditch around your house that is twice as wide as a concrete block and about 0.5 metres (1.5 feet) deep. Fill this ditch with concrete and wait at least 24 hours before beginning the wall building. The appropriate mix for wall foundations is 1 part cement, 2.5 parts sand and 3.5 parts gravel. Mix in some water until you achieve a uniform consistency.

After 24 hours go and check the foundation to see if it has set properly. Do this by applying some pressure on the foundation with your finger. If the foundation feels rock solid then you are ready to begin building the first section of wall. If it feels in any way squishy then leave it set for a further 24 hours. Mix the concrete for the walls with 1 part concrete and 2 parts sand. Make sure that the wall is built level and only build up to 3 blocks high on day one. Wait for 24 hours and build a further 3 blocks high. Continue this process until the wall is 3 metres (10 feet) high.

The plastic piping that you get should have the biggest diameter possible. Cut a section out of the full length of the pipe that is exactly as wide as a concrete block. The fit should be as tight as possible to ensure that it will not fall off the wall during an attack. Fit the plastic piping to the top of the wall. You may need to use a lot of force to get the pipe to fit properly. Apply a generous amount of axle grease to all sides of the plastic pipe.

This type of wall should be sufficient for repelling zombies but it is still good practice to always enhance your defences whenever possible. If you come across razor wire you can add this to the outside, inside or on top of the wall to add an extra layer of protection.

Booby traps

WARNING: Booby traps can kill. It is **not** a good idea to practice making these lethal traps before the zombie apocalypse. In most countries around the world, it is illegal to make some of these traps and you could end up in prison even if nobody is injured or killed by the trap.

If you decide to build booby traps around your property they should be built outside your defensive wall to minimise the possibility of you or a member of your party activating them by accident. It is up to you whether or not to place some kind of warning sign so humans can be aware of their existence and thus avoid the area. You may be under constant and repeated attacks from a gang of humans but if you are not it is important to warn others. If you ever decide to abandon your house you should deactivate all booby traps to prevent others from being injured or killed. Ensure that all people in your house or encampment are fully aware of the dangers of these booby traps and where they are located. A good idea would be to keep a journal of all booby trap locations around your house with sketches. These sketches should also contain detailed measurements.

Some of the best booby traps will involve explosives. If you can get your hands on some claymore mines, position these around your property. These mines have an effective range of approximately 50 metres (165 feet) and fire steel pellets in a 60^0 arc in front of the device resulting in a high kill rate. Place claymore mines at least 20 meters (65 feet) away from your perimeter walls as there is a danger of back blast. Only a tiny amount of people will have access to claymore mines during the zombie apocalypse, with the purchase and possession of these weapons being illegal to non-military organisations in every country on Earth but they are mentioned here for their unbelievable ability as a defensive weapon.

A more realistic and affordable booby trap is bear traps. These are easy, yet dangerous, to set up and cause severe injuries to anyone who sets them off. Bear traps work similar to mouse traps in that a pressure plate needs to be activated in order for sharpened steel teeth on either side of the trap close at a fast speed. Use extreme caution when setting these traps as they can unexpectedly activate and have the power to break bones or even sever a limb.

Punji pits were used very effectively by the Viet Cong during the Vietnam War. A punji pit is simply a pit filled with large sharp spikes and covered in order to camouflage their position from the enemy. To build a punji pit begin by digging a large hole in the ground that is approximately 1 metre (3 feet) x 1 meter (3 feet) with a depth of approximately 1.5 meters (5 feet). You can always build smaller traps if materials are scarce or you don't have time for building large traps. Sharpen several sticks and secure these in the base of the hole with the sharp end facing up. Place some small sticks across the opening and sprinkle dirt and leaves over these sticks in order to camouflage the punji pit.

Dangers

During the zombie apocalypse, you will face dangers on a nearly constant basis. In time things may settle down a bit but during the first few years, you will face a torrent of dangers. These dangers will push you to your limits but for every danger you successfully face you will learn a little bit more about how to avoid them or face them head on.

Zombies

Zombies will be everywhere. They will essentially be human beings but with the added benefit of not being able to feel any pain or suffer from climate considerations such as very cold or very hot temperatures. They will be consumed by a violent blood lust rage and will immediately attack on sight.

The dead will not be able to re-animate into zombies. Once they are dead they will stay dead. Do not believe what you see in movies or TV shows about the dead coming back to life. If you kill a human being during this time they will not turn into a zombie.

Unlike the portrayal of zombies in movies and TV shows, they will be able to complete some basic tasks such as opening doors or windows in order to gain entry to your house. They will look like any other person but may be distinguished by their lack of a gun, backpack or other supplies. Expect these zombies to be able to use knives and other stabbing weapons. A gun may be too complex for them and they will never be seen driving cars or other vehicles.

These zombies will not feel pain and are difficult to kill. Once they set their sights on you, they will not stop their attack until you stop them. If a group of zombies find out where you are hiding expect them to ruthlessly attack your stronghold and continue their assault night and day until they gain entry.

You may not be able to identify a zombie until you are up close to them. They may be walking around like a normal human but once they begin to run at you, they will not stop. Zombies can starve to death in the same amount of time as a human and are susceptible to death due to a lack of water in the same way a human would be.

It will not be possible to reverse the zombie condition. Zombies will not be able to spread their disease in any traditional manner that we are accustomed to. If they bite you, you will not turn into one of them.

Other people

Remember that everyone wants to survive. Just like you, they are willing to do just about anything to ensure their survival and the survival of their family. If you encounter another person while you are away from your house make sure that you keep your weapon trained on them at all times. Ask them what they want and warn them to leave the area. Do not allow these people to see you returning to your house as they may follow you and ambush you at a later stage when your guard is down.

If people approach you with an offer to trade some products you must be very cautious when engaging in this trade. Ensure that nobody sees where your stash of supplies is and only arrange a trade on your terms and not theirs. Always come armed and ready to attack. It may be possible, and in some cases necessary, to link up with another group of people but that will not happen through one meeting and will take a significant amount of time to build enough trust. Never let your guard down for any reason.

Animals

Nature has a habit of reclaiming any territory that humans abandon. The only thing that keeps animals out of cities and towns is consistent human activity. Once most of the human population has been killed off wild animals will begin to patrol through cities in a search for food. Even domestic dogs will begin to gather in wild packs as they are abandoned by their owners. Wild instincts in dogs will become dominant. A pack of wild dogs can easily kill you.

Most people have never encountered a dangerous wild animal such as bears, wild cats, wolves, snakes, etc. Keep a constant watch for any wild animals and keep out of their way as any encounter could become fatal. If you come across a wild animal it will initially be as shocked as you are. When you come across a wild animal immediately freeze. Do not move a muscle. Begin talking in a calm manner and very slowly back away from the animal. Keep control of your breathing and do your best not to get yourself worked into a panicked state. If, after backing away, the animal charges you, it is best to run for cover as fast as you can move. Some large animals such as bears can be shot multiple times and still maintain their charge. You will **not** win a fight against a bear.

Other animals and insects

Many small creatures and insects that were considered only a nuisance before the zombie apocalypse can quickly become a major problem. What if you are allergic to wasp stings? Normally you would go to a hospital or use an epinephrine injection if stung, but this may no longer be possible. Hornets have been known to kill people.

Imagine contracting malaria from a mosquito bite in these apocalyptic times. This can land you in a lot of trouble. Even if a creature's sting is not fatal it can put you in a world of pain that could last for hours or days. Such pain will greatly hinder your ability to gather water or food. It will become increasingly difficult to defend yourself from attacks.

Common domestic dogs will form packs that can be very dangerous if you encounter them. You may find yourself under attack from 20 or more dogs. If you are under such an attack the only thing that could save you is to frighten them by firing a gun or setting off a loud personal alarm. The pack will back off and you must get up and run before they gather again for another attack.

If you live in Indonesia you need to be aware of Komodo dragons. These lizards will stalk you until they get a chance to bite. Once they bite you they will retreat but this isn't the end of the attack. A Komodo dragon's mouth is swimming with bacteria and that bite will become badly infected and result in putting you out of commission. That's when the Komodo dragon will return and eat you.

Poisonous snakes and scorpions can cause either severe damage or death and should be avoided at all costs. Remember that any creature you stumble upon will initially be just as shocked as you are. Back away immediately.

If you live in swamp areas that contain crocodiles or alligators they will begin to encroach on your territory as more humans die or evacuate your neighbourhood. These creatures are very dangerous and should be avoided wherever possible. If the populations of these creatures are climbing to an uncontrollable level it may be best to abandon your house and migrate to a new location. It may not be possible to fully cull crocodile or alligator populations.

Everyday insects such as flies could present a major problem if they get into your food supplies. Flies can spread diseases such as typhoid, dysentery, salmonella, anthrax and cholera to name just a few. Common house flies can multiply rapidly, especially in warm climates, and must be eradicated as soon as possible.

Epidemics

When infectious diseases rapidly spread to large numbers of people it becomes an epidemic. Infections such as bubonic plague, smallpox, yellow fever, cholera, Ebola and influenza can, and will, cause widespread devastation during the zombie apocalypse. Normally those who are affected will be quarantined in hospitals and treated for the infection but as hospitals are no longer operating epidemics will spread very fast.

Some people will possess a natural immunity to different infections and these people will survive untouched, but most of those affected could die depending on the mortality rate of the virus they contract.

Should you become struck down by an infection it is important in the early days of illness to gather as much food and water to your bedside as you won't be able to do this at a later stage. Arrange for sufficient warmth being available in your bedroom during the time that you will be confined to your bed. If you are alone then you can only hope that zombies or humans do not come across your house while you are sick. If you are in a group it is vital that you quarantine the infected as soon as possible in order to stop the spread of infection.

Unseen dangers

Just like the modern world we currently live in, dangers can manifest in many different ways. A truck could crash through your home. An aeroplane could hit your house. A meteorite could crash through our atmosphere and hit you on the head, killing you instantly.

There is no way to predict what kind of unseen danger could come your way, that's why it is vital to always be prepared for anything and everything. Always stay on alert and pay close attention to any signs around you, such as animals acting strangely or *"the quiet before the storm"*.

Your first instinct will usually be the correct one. When something unexpected occurs you will usually be faced with two choices, stay or run. This will need to be decided in a split second. The only way to make the correct choice is to be prepared and know as much as you can about survival, the general area you are in and how to evade an enemy.

Shelter

When it comes to shelter you may think that it is best to stay in your own home. After all, that's where you feel safe, right? Well, it depends. Do you live in a city, suburban area, small town, or in any form of an urban area?

WARNING: Do not stay in any form of built up urban area or you will die.

In an urban area, you will be subjected to attacks from zombies and other humans but the most dangerous attack will come from the very people who arrive and promise to take you to a safe and secure area for your own protection. Those people who should be taking care of you are your own military. Every house or dwelling in your country is registered somewhere and will eventually be visited in order to take you away. Whatever dwelling you choose you may need to abandon it for a short period of time while the military sweep through the area.

Temporary shelters

You may find yourself on the run and living in a tent or in a makeshift shelter in a natural gully, drainage tunnel, etc. These types of shelters will provide you with absolutely zero defence against attacks and should be only used as a last resort.

If you must stay in a temporary shelter then do the best you can to camouflage its location and keep noise and light pollution to an absolute minimum in order to hide you from zombies and other humans.

Caves

Caves have the potential to be some of the best areas to stay. Deep caves tend to have a constant temperature based on the average annual temperature of the local area. Caves do not automatically draw the attention of military or zombies. Defence may become a major issue when dealing with caves especially if there is only one entrance, as you will not have an escape route. The entrance to a cave can be easily hidden with vegetation in order to minimise the possibility of being discovered.

Houses

The best type of house to occupy is one that is fully detached and located outside any major city or town. It should still be within half a day walking distance from a major shopping centre or other shopping area. Ideally, there will be a stream and a large wooden area nearby. The woods can provide food, timber and a hiding place when needed.

If the house already has a perimeter wall, even a low wall, this has potential to be a good defensible area. Solar panels or a wind generation system, a perimeter wall, a stream, a wooded area and being fully detached will make this a very high-value safe haven.

High rise buildings

These types of buildings will be very difficult to defend and could easily become a death-trap, not only from zombies but from dangers such as other humans, fire, disease, etc. As most, if not all high-rise buildings are located in large cities you could easily find yourself trapped due to the amount of zombies on the streets. In this scenario, if you run out of food you will either need to face the zombies outside or starve to death. An added danger in these areas will be military forces passing through and rounding up people. Due to the technology that soldiers will possess during these searches, you will be found no matter how well you hide from them.

Underground bunker

Underground bunkers are possibly one of the best places to be but only if there are sufficient supplies to last for up to 5 years. Theoretically, you could survive in underground bunkers very comfortably for a long time without needing to expose yourself to danger by going outside.

Unfortunately, you may be lulling yourself into a false sense of security as these bunkers will become targets for the military. They want your supplies and they want your bunker. No matter how well you try to hide an underground bunker the military will find it in a very short time. If you are lucky they will simply throw you out of the bunker but it is more than likely that you will be taken away to a large holding facility. Your chances of surviving in these facilities will drop to zero.

Starting a Fire

The ability to start a fire is vital for cooking food, boiling water or generally keeping you warm. It can be used for drying out food for preservation or drying clothes. You could set up a complex defensive system that includes a moat filled with flammable fuels but if you can't start a fire it will become useless. Starting a fire is one of the skills that you **must** master if you are to survive.

To be safe when dealing with a fire, ensure that you place stones around the area where your fire will be lighting. This will stop the fire from spreading throughout your campground but will also heat up the rocks. These heated rocks can be used later as a makeshift hot water bottle or another heat source. The residual heat in these rocks will not last long but could be the difference between life and death.

Always exercise caution with having a fire as the flames, light or smoke could draw the attention of zombies or undesirable humans. When lighting a fire in your house be aware that smoke will rise from your chimney and could be visible from quite a distance.

Shops and hardware stores can provide large stores of lighting material such as firewood or coal. If at all possible, stock up on these items. During the summer months begin storing fire materials for when winter comes. If you are lucky you may stumble upon a massive store of lighters and matches. If you do, take as many as possible back to your house and store these safely. Do not waste gas from lighters or matches and only use them when absolutely necessary.

WARNING: Starting a fire inside your house without adequate ventilation can lead to a build-up of carbon monoxide which can kill very quickly. Always ensure that there is sufficient ventilation and clean your chimney regularly if you can. It is always best to build a fire outside but this has the drawback of potentially drawing unwanted attention.

Petroleum

Most petroleum fuels, petrol, diesel, etc. contain preservatives that will break down after 1 year. This means that you will only have the use of petroleum based vehicles for only 1 year. After this time the fuel will begin to break-down and become lumpy. It should still remain flammable for up to 2 years after it begins to break-down. This will be one of the easiest fuel sources for keeping a fire burning but you will need to start a fire first. Do not add too many materials too quickly as this could extinguish the flame.

Flint

Flint lighters are designed to create a spark only. In a butane lighter, this spark will ignite the gas, producing a usable flame. But what do you do if you only have the flint but no gas? You will need to gather dry tinder, wool or light tissue paper. Use the flint to create sparks that will light this starter material. Once this material is smouldering it is important to gently blow on the embers to encourage the material to take light more effectively. Once a suitable flame is established begin adding more flammable material and eventually firewood or coal to the fire. Do not add too many materials too quickly as this could extinguish the flame.

Magnifying glass

If you're lucky enough to live in a sunny climate you can easily use a magnifying glass to start a fire. Gather some dry tinder, wool or light tissue paper and hold the magnifying glass in such a way that the light passes through it and onto your material. Move the magnifying glass closer or further away until you get the smallest point of light on your lighting material. It will take between a few seconds and a few minutes for the material to ignite. Blow gently on this until a fire takes hold and add more flammable material until eventually, you are able to add firewood or coal. Do not add too many materials too quickly as this could extinguish the flame.

By hand

To use this method you must first ensure that **all** materials are bone dry. If anything is damp then don't waste your valuable energy on attempting this method. Find a wooden board that has a split in the middle or that is missing a knot which forms a natural depression in the wood. If this is not possible take a wooden board and cut out a section from the centre. Take a piece of circular wood such as a section of a tree branch and sharpen one end into a point.

Place some tinder, wool or light tissue paper into the depression and roll the sharpened piece of wood between your hands, with the sharpened point in the centre of the tinder and touching the wooden board. Continue rolling the sharpened piece of wood until the friction causes the tinder to begin glowing. Once this happens, stop and gently blow on the material until fire takes hold and add more flammable material until eventually, you are able to add firewood or coal. Do not add too many materials too quickly as this could extinguish the flame.

Hygiene

Your general hygiene is absolutely vital for keeping your spirits up during these dark and turbulent times. Keeping yourself clean will also help in keeping your exposure to illness due to disease at bay.

General hygiene

If your water supply is limited do not have a shower or fully wash yourself. Instead, make sure that you keep some fresh water for washing your hands. You should wash your hands after going to the toilet, preparing food, handling animals and before consuming a meal. Always wash your hands before going to sleep as you will move during the night and may scratch at your face or touch your mouth.

When your water supply is plentiful take full advantage of this by fully washing your body. Set up a makeshift shower or use solar panels to power an electric shower. Be aware that electric showers are very loud and could draw the attention of zombies or undesirable humans to your location.

If you are able to get supplies from a store or shopping centre you could stock up on toiletries like shampoo, soap, etc. and hand sanitizer. If you have a ready supply of or are able to get a supply of razor blades, shaving regularly can boost your sense of well-being.

Rubbish disposal

All generated rubbish should be disposed of properly. The garbage collection service, like all public services, will no longer operate once a zombie apocalypse has taken hold. You could bring your rubbish a good distance from your house and dump it, however, this can be dangerous and the pile of rubbish could alert someone that there are people, with supplies, alive in the general area. An alternative option would be to dump your rubbish a shorter distance from your home by digging a very large pit or use a natural gully, that is closer, easier to get to, and safer to get to.

Incinerator

An incinerator is a great way of disposing of your rubbish but be aware that any smoke generated could draw the attention of zombies or humans. If you are any way technically inclined you may be able to construct a power-generating incinerator at your house before the zombie apocalypse. This gives you the added benefit of not only disposing of your waste but also generating electrical power. Such an incinerator could even provide heat to your house.

Disposing of dead bodies

During the zombie apocalypse, there is going to be a considerable amount of dead bodies lying around. Regardless of how they died, you must not allow these bodies to decompose anywhere near you or your house. If your water supply is derived from a nearby stream, a decomposing body in this stream can spread disease. If possible take the body a minimum of 200 metres (656 feet) from your house and bury it. If burying is not an option you can place thick plastic sacks around the body and cover it with a heavy porous lining such as a carpet or rug.

Ensure that you fully wash immediately after handling a dead body. If you have bleach at hand dilute this and use it as an initial wash. If you do use bleach be sure to rinse yourself thoroughly.

Unlike fictional zombies depicted in movies and TV shows, the dead **will not** re-animate and become a zombie. The only thing to fear from the dead is disease and possibly a few nightmares.

Healthcare and First Aid

During the zombie apocalypse, you will need to become your own doctor and emergency medic. Regular civilian medical infrastructure such as doctor's surgeries, dentists and hospitals will fail. During the early days of the apocalypse, hospitals will prove to be death traps for anyone who gathers at them. Apart from the world's medical system being overrun to the point of collapse, they will be high priority target areas for zombies. There is also a good chance that you could walk in the front door only to be herded out the back door and into transport trucks by the military.

I would strongly suggest that you prepare now for looking after yourself in the future. Take private first aid lessons or join your local Civil Defence group, as they will teach you for free. I can't possibly detail every type of medical procedure that you will need to know but I will list some below.

General First aid

When dealing with first aid it is important to carefully consider your priorities. For example, if you have a group and one of the members has been in a bad accident or attacked resulting in several broken bones, bleeding, etc. and you begin treating their wounds but they are not breathing then they will die. You will need to get them breathing again before dealing with other wounds.

Immediate priorities are:

- Airway
- Breathing
- Circulation

Is their airway blocked? This needs to be cleared first. Are they breathing? If not, you need to begin CPR. Is blood circulation through their system? That can only happen if their heart is beating. If their heart is not beating, you will need to begin CPR immediately.

If many people in your group are injured, use the above priority list to determine who you will treat first. Someone with a small gash or minor fracture should be ignored in favour of treating someone who is not breathing.

The best way to put first aid into action is to first know how and what to do. This kind of training can **only** be gained before the zombie apocalypse by attending first aid courses. Don't wait for the event to happen, be prepared for it.

Bleeding and stitching wounds

You only have a limited amount of blood in your system and without a blood transfusion it takes a long time for your body to replace any blood loss. If you get a deep cut that causes any bleeding you must take immediate steps to stem the flow of blood. Apply pressure to the affected area in order for the blood to clot around the wound. Clean the area with fresh water and bandage up the wound with a clean dry dressing.

If you sever an artery, blood will be lost at an extremely rapid rate and, if you are on your own, will most likely result in death. Apply pressure to the wound and bandage as above. Get yourself into a comfortable position. Tilt your head to the side as you will most likely vomit. You will eventually go into a coma and ultimately die.

To stitch a wound, first clean it thoroughly with clean fresh water and stitch the wound just like stitching a piece of clothing. Ensure that both sides of the wound are touching each other once you have finished stitching. The wound will begin to heal and you should monitor this repair closely. Once the wound appears to be healed enough to hold together on its own you can remove the stitches. Wounds can be stitched with thread or fishing line but first, make sure that all materials are sterilised to minimise the risk of infection.

Burns

If you suffer any burns during the apocalypse you will need to treat these quickly in order to minimise the possibility of shock and infection. Burns, even small burns, will result in severe pain and fluid loss.

To treat a burn, saturate the area with fresh cold water. Only use water, unless you have a specific medical burn treatment substance that is still within its sell-by date. Dress the wound with clean dry dressings. It is imperative that you replace these dressings every day with fresh ones. If you are out of bandages you can cut up clean sterile T-shirts in order to create your own homemade dressings.

You will need to drink more water than normal in order to replace the fluids that are lost because of the burns. Drink small amounts on a regular basis. Don't neglect this step as it is vital to your survival.

As a general rule, if the burns are covering more than half of your body you will not survive without a hospital. A post-apocalyptic hospital will not be able to help you at this stage, only a present day facility that has electrical power and sufficient equipment and staff would be able to offer any help. If your burns are this severe you will need to make yourself as comfortable as possible. If you still possess any pain killers it is time to take them. If you are lucky you may slip into unconsciousness before you die.

Broken bones

There are two types of breaks, a closed and an open break. A closed break means that the bone is broken with no wounds on the outside of the skin. An open break is the most dangerous and these result in the broken piece of bone breaking through the skin and becoming visible.

The most painful part of dealing with broken bones is setting the break back in place. You will need to pull the affected limb until both ends of the break line up. Then apply splints on either side of the limb and tie these in place. The idea is to keep both ends of the break as close to each other as possible, similar to stitching a wound. Both ends will begin to reattach and heal over time.

It is possible, during the setting process that you may trap a nerve with part of the broken bone. This will result in excruciating pain and must be corrected immediately. The only way to correct this is to reset the break again. You may need to reset the break several times in order to stop the nerve being trapped. I hope you have pain killers available to you.

It is very important to immobilise the limb, the less movement of the limb, the less likely that the two ends of the break will separate and interrupt the healing process. If your arm is broken you will need to create a sling and tie this around your neck. If the break is in your leg you will need to splint this in a straight orientation.

All broken bones will result in extreme inconvenience in your daily survival activities. Different bones will take different times to heal and could ultimately take up to 10 weeks to fully heal. You will need to adjust the way you survive during this time.

Shock

Shock is life-threatening and must be identified and treated now. If you identify the symptoms of shock in a member of your group or yourself you must stop everything you are doing and make this a top priority. Shock can manifest due to severe injuries or a severe illness and results in insufficient blood flow around the body.

Some of the symptoms of shock include:

- Cold, clammy skin
- Rapid pulse
- Shallow breathing
- Weakness
- 1,000-yard stare (the casualty is staring through you and cannot focus on you)
- Sweating
- Chest pains
- Confusion
- Anxiety
- Seizures
- Blue lips (due to oxygen deprivation)

There may be very little that you can do to treat this if you do not have access to medicines, a doctor or medic, or medical equipment. If you have no supplies of any kind it is best to stay warm and drink a large amount of water over a short period of time in an attempt to raise your blood pressure. If you have access to IV equipment administer this IV in order to replenish any lost fluids.

Medicines

Just like foodstuffs, medicines have a limited sell-by-date. Also, after water and food, medicines will be the most looted items and could become difficult to come across.

If you are able to gather medical supplies always be aware that these will not last indefinitely. Just like every other product they will have a sell-by date.

Painkillers will probably be the most sought after medical supply and as a result, these may be difficult to find. The most effective painkiller is Morphine but it is also the most dangerous. It is very easy to overdose on Morphine with even tiny amounts of the drug. Also, Morphine will quickly knock you out of commission and render you unable to fight or defend yourself from attack.

If you do not have any pain killers then there is something you can do to minimise the pain. Visualising the pain away is a fantastic start. While it won't instantly take the pain away it will help give you the drive to get out of bed and carry on with your survival. To visualise the pain away just lie down or sit down where you feel the most comfortable, in your bed, on a chair, etc. Make sure that all possible distractions are removed from your attention and that your doors, windows, etc. are secured.

Close your eyes and take several deep breaths. Relax all of your muscles. You could do this by imagining yourself floating in a beautiful pool on a sunny day. When you feel relaxed enough imagine that the pool slowly transforms into your bed, or the chair you are sitting on. In your mind imagine every aspect of your room. Now imagine that you jump out of bed feeling very invigorated and happy about the day ahead. In your mind, you go about your morning routine feeling absolutely fantastic and pain-free. In your mind, you can clearly feel that today is going to be a great one with no pain, or zombies, or violent humans, or soldiers. Now jump to a scene of you working on building up your defences. You are easily able to work with no pain of any kind.

The reason for doing all this is that the brain cannot distinguish between your visualisation and real life. As far as your brain is concerned they are the same thing. Your brain will want to live out this fantastic pain-free day that you visualised and will do everything in its power to make sure that happens. Now open your eyes, jump out of bed and live out that fantastic pain-free day.

Most people in emergency situations like the zombie apocalypse will overlook antibiotics. While they are sometimes an absolute necessity they can also be bad for you and should never be taken for every sniffle or pain. It may become impossible for you to be able to determine when to take an antibiotic. You will need to use your best judgment on this one. The best possible advice is to immediately stop taking an antibiotic if you develop a rash or any other bad reaction. If you are taking an antibiotic and your condition is improving than continue the course for two weeks. You may feel better after a few days but antibiotics will take two weeks to fully eliminate the infection.

Some antibiotics and what infections they treat:

- Ciprofloxacin (urinary tract, bacterial diarrhoea)
- Metronidazole (brain abscesses, meningitis)
- Cephalexin (Bronchitis, pneumonia, ear infections)
- Erythromycin (Lyme disease, chlamydia)
- Doxycycline (Typhus, malaria)
- Sulfamethoxazole combined with Trimethoprim (MRSA)

You will need to do a considerable amount of research about antibiotics before even considering treating yourself or someone else with these. Remember, doctors study for up to 8 years before they are allowed to practice. Do not randomly take medications without knowing exactly what they do, what they treat and what symptoms must be present before using them. An allergic reaction to medications can quickly result in death.

Heatstroke

During the summer months, it is possible to suffer from heatstroke, especially if you are very busy building defences all day and have little water or shade. If left untreated, heatstroke can cause damage to your brain, heart and kidneys that could quickly result in death.

Some of the symptoms of heatstroke include:

- High body temperature
- Confusion
- Irritability
- Seizures
- Nausea
- Vomiting
- Rapid breathing
- Dramatically increased heart rate
- Severe headaches
- Flushed skin

In today's relatively safe environment it is easy to treat heatstroke by cooling down in air conditioned buildings and by taking nice cold drinks from the fridge. However, during the zombie apocalypse, you most likely do not have access to air conditioning or a working fridge. If you notice that you are suffering from heatstroke get indoors and under shade immediately. Take off all of your clothes and sponge yourself with cold water. If you have a makeshift shower available get under cold water. Wet some towels or small pieces of clothing and place these on your forehead, neck, armpits and wrists. Continue applying water and dampened cloth until all symptoms are gone. Rest for as long as possible before beginning any physical activities again. Rehydrate by drinking plenty of fluids.

Hypothermia

Hypothermia is when your body's core temperature drops to a dangerously low level. Perhaps you have a house with loads of drafts and you have been out in cold weather all day and maybe you have gotten wet during the day and maybe you have no ability to start a fire. This can quickly result in hypothermia and you are at imminent risk of death.

The biggest problem with hypothermia is that you may not recognise that you are suffering from it because it will make you very confused and even give you a false sense that you are warm. Some hypothermia victims have been found dead in freezing conditions while naked. At the later stages, they believed they were very warm and removed their clothing.

If you are on your own, in very cold conditions where you are shivering from the cold, and find that you have now stopped shivering even though you are still in a very cold area, then you may be suffering from the early stages and you should seek emergency shelter and warmth immediately. Replace any wet clothes with dry ones and make a hot beverage to sip on. This will help with warming your core from the inside.

Mental Health

Your mental health is just as important as your physical health and may be very difficult to sustain efficiently throughout the zombie apocalypse. In ordinary everyday life, we encounter many stresses and strains that lead to some people having full mental breakdowns.

There are some things that you will be able to do in order to keep you mentally sound. Build a regular daily routine that includes at least 30 minutes of game time such as; playing card games or other board games. Keeping warm and well hydrated goes a long way to boosting your mood.

Keep a journal

Keeping a journal is useful for tracking your mood as well as keeping notes about possible food and water supplies, dangerous areas, etc. Write in your journal every day about your current mood. If you are feeling down at a specific time during each day then you may be able to find a common cause for this and ultimately change the way you think about this which in turn could put a stop to these bad feelings.

Gratitude

Being grateful for things in your life works wonders for boosting your mood no matter how bad things are going in your life. You could be grateful for anything. You're limbs that allow you to build your defences every day, the fact that you are still alive, your food supplies, your water supplies, your house, anything.

The best way to begin being grateful is to write down a list of things that you are grateful for (if you have paper and pens).

Take a few minutes every day to list down at least 3 things that you are grateful for. After a day or two, you will notice that you have far more than just 3 things to add to your list every day. You will notice that your mood improves and things just seem a lot better in life. If you want to, you can go over your list of things to be grateful for in your mind while you are going about your daily tasks. Don't get too wrapped up in this thinking because you will still need to keep your wits about you and watch out for danger.

It has been discovered that if you are trying to think of things you are grateful for it forces your brain to release serotonin. Serotonin is responsible for maintaining your mood balance and a lack of serotonin can cause depression. Some antidepressants function by chemically increasing the serotonin levels in the brain.

Give immense amounts of gratitude for everything. Any time you find some supplies in a shop or an abandoned stash of supplies feel extremely grateful for your good fortune. If you manage to make it through a full day without encountering a zombie or a violent human or the military, then as you go to sleep that night give immense gratitude for this great day.

PTSD

Post-Traumatic Stress Disorder will become a big problem in this new apocalyptic world. You will see things that currently only exist in the worst of horror movies and you will see these things on a daily basis.

Danger will be an active part of your life for a considerable length of time before things begin to settle down a bit.

PTSD will not strike during a traumatic event. Rather, it will manifest days, weeks, months or even years after the event.

Some of the symptoms of PTSD include:

- Playing out the traumatic event, over and over in your mind
- Increased anxiety
- Panic attacks manifesting under non-stressful situations
- Recurring nightmares related to the event
- Losing your survival mindset and believing that you won't last another day
- Feeling emotionally numb
- Insomnia
- Extreme difficulty in concentrating on anything
- Being easily startled and staying on alert, even in obviously safe situations
- Survivors guilt (feeling guilty that you lived when others died)

When you are suffering from PTSD your nervous system has been badly pushed off balance. In today's relatively safe world the best way to combat PTSD is to spend time having social interactions with others. If you have other people in your group just talk with them or play card games in the evenings and generally try to have fun.

If however, you are on your own in this new world then you will need to engage with a mood altering activity such as exercising. When you exercise your brain will release endorphins.

Endorphins are the feel good drug that makes us happy. But how does your brain create a connection between exercise and the release of endorphins? When you engage in intensive exercise the primitive part of your brain will interpret this as a moment of stress more commonly known as the fight or flight response. Your brain thinks that you are in imminent danger. The sole purpose of endorphins being released into your system is to block out pain and to put your mind into a state of euphoria. Seems strange that the brain would do this as a response to what it perceives as danger, right? The reason has to do with the brain's self-preservation mechanism. Your brain doesn't know that you are exercising; it thinks that you are desperately trying to escape from some unseen danger. But what if this unseen danger was to catch up with you and kill you? The brain does not want to face death, this is the reason it goes into a state of euphoria, just in case the worst should happen. By exercising vigorously you are fooling the brain into releasing the feel good drug into your system. Another fantastic effect of vigorous exercise (which your brain interprets as imminent danger) is that a protein called Brain-Derived Neurotrophic Factor is released as part of the self-preservation mechanism that will reset your memory neurones. Basically, your brain resets itself so that all unnecessary distractions are forgotten about so that the brain can focus exclusively on surviving this unseen danger. This protein is the reason that you will feel at ease, peaceful and content after doing some form of vigorous exercise because all of your worries are forgotten for a brief time.

I know this sounds strange and counterintuitive, to fool the brain into thinking it is in danger in order to recover from a traumatic event that was more than likely related to a real life-threatening danger, but this does indeed work for getting rid of PTSD.

Get up every morning and set about reinforcing and increasing your defences around your house. Take a break for lunch and end your busy day at dinner time. Doing this for several days will cause your mood to start changing from one of anxiousness to one of feeling calm.

Clothing

Your clothes can mean the difference between life and death during any survival situation. If you wear shorts and a T-shirt during freezing temperatures you will not survive very long. Sufficient camouflage is vital also to ensure that you do not draw undue attention to yourself. Zombies will mostly respond to sudden movements more than colour. Humans will respond to movement as well as bright colours. It may not be practical to attain camouflage clothing for each specific environment that you encounter. The best general colour to wear, that provides an all-around camouflage, is grey. Avoid bright colours like red, blue, yellow or white.

If you get the chance, visit a clothing store and take as many clothes, in your size, as you can. The more trips you take to a store the more likely it is that you will come under attack.

Simple everyday tasks such as hanging your clothes out to dry can, during the zombie apocalypse, result in drawing unwanted attention that could lead to your death. If possible, segregate a room in your house to be used for washing and drying clothes.

Waterproofing

Waterproofing clothes is important for not only keeping the water out but also for expanding the lifespan of your clothes. Even if you have secured a massive stockpile of clothes, that could last you several lifetimes, you will need to do waterproofing because you don't know if you will lose your supplies in the future or if you will go on the run. There is no need to waterproof everything, just those items that will be exposed, such as jackets, pants and boots.

If you can get your hands on spray sealers take as many of these as you can. If the item of clothing is dirty you will need to clean it first. Ensure that the piece of clothing is thoroughly dry before spraying or it might not adhere correctly leaving spots that are not protected. Make sure the area you are working in is well ventilated and spray on the sealant in accordance with the instructions on the can. Apply two coats of waterproofing spray and wait until it is thoroughly dry before using the piece of clothing.

If you can't find any waterproofing spray you can use a bar of natural beeswax. Heat up the bar of beeswax and rub it across the piece of clothing in both horizontal and vertical directions to ensure that all areas are covered.

Linseed oil can also be used for waterproofing clothes. Whatever method you choose don't forget to waterproof your boots as wet feet can quickly cool you down and can also cause you to easily develop trench foot if your feet remain wet for an extended period of time.

Footwear

In the coming post-apocalyptic era, normal shoes or trainers just won't be acceptable footwear because they will not last very long. The best type of boots to have is heavyweight hiking boots as these will give you very good ankle support and can be used in all types of terrains. These are usually expensive and only sold in specialised hiking stores. If you can raid a nearby hiking store take as many pairs as possible. It is absolutely vital to take boots in your exact size as boots that are too small or too big will eventually do damage to your feet, leg muscles or even your spine.

All of the boots you gather **must** be broken-in properly or you could quickly find yourself suffering from blisters and sore muscles. Let's say you gather 20 pairs of boots. Over the next 20 days wear each pair to ensure that they are all broken-in. The reason for this is that you may put on a brand new pair of boots one morning and your house may be attacked. If you go on the run with these new boots that are not properly broken-in, you will not get very far before foot problems emerge. When on the run you will need to be able to comfortably move fast for potentially days on end.

Ensure that you waterproof your boots as soon as possible and clean them whenever possible. If you do any work on the outside of your property or hike in a muddy area it is important to regularly clear the threads at the end of the boots of any mud or debris. Otherwise, the boots will become slippery and impede your ability to outrun danger or climb effectively.

Laces have a tendency to break easily after only a short time. If you are ever raiding a store in the future keep an eye out for extra laces and take as many as you can carry.

Protective clothing

By protective clothing, I don't mean hi-visibility jackets or safety harnesses. I mean things that can afford a good level of protection from injuries that could easily put you out of commission. The best type of protection for raiding stores, attacking zombies or defending your house will, of course, be bulletproof vests, Kevlar helmets and stab vests. The possibility of you getting your hands on these advanced bulletproof materials may be remote but there are some things you can do.

If you are on the move, defending your house or going on a raid you can wear 2 large jackets as well as 2 large jumpers. This will afford at least some protection from knives. Wearing kneepads and elbow pads can save you from injuries from falls or injuries sustained from climbing, etc. The more layers of protection you wear will greatly aid in protecting you, however, this, in turn, will hinder your ability to move, fight and climb.

A protective helmet of some kind will certainly protect you from things that are falling or things that are being thrown at you. If you come across a dead fireman or abandoned fire truck check to see if there are any helmets lying around and take one.

If you find yourself in a firefight and you are decked out from head to toe in Kevlar bulletproof gear this is still not a guarantee that a bullet will not get through. Any time you come under fire you must keep your head down and never expose yourself to the line of fire. Rather than stay and fight you should, at all costs, hide, evade and eventually run.

Sewing kit

If you don't know how to sew on a button how are you expected to know how to sew up a wound? This is something that you can practice long before the zombie apocalypse comes to pass. You will need several sized needles, thread, a very sharp small scissors and a thimble. The reason for the thimble is that you can push needles through though materials without impaling your thumb. Sewing can be used for not only replacing buttons on garments but also for repairing tears in clothes, boots, bedding, etc.

Travel

Travel will become as vital a component during the zombie apocalypse as it is today. All public transport systems will fail such as underground trains, buses, etc. It will become very difficult to drive as roads will contain military and police roadblocks, whether manned or not, and abandoned vehicles. Ambushes will become a constant danger and you will need to look out for these at all times while travelling anywhere.

Maintain extreme caution when someone shows up and offers you a lift or wants your help retrieving a vehicle. Once they have you in a car they have you. Always think strategically in everything you do as this could mean you can live for another day.

Transport

You will still be able to use normal cars and trucks for up to one year after the beginning of the zombie apocalypse. The best type of vehicle to use is one with a low cc (to conserve fuel), is four-wheel drive (to get over obstacles and difficult terrain) and has enough trunk space to carry any looted supplies. The quieter the vehicle the better as any kind of noise could bring you unwanted attention. You may decide to disable the horn on the vehicle so that you do not accidentally trigger it at the wrong time. You might think it would be a good idea to fit metal plates all over your vehicle in order to protect yourself while on the move; however, this added weight may render your vehicle useless.

You will need to find, at some stage, an alternative form of transport as petroleum fuels will not last very long. If you can find an electric vehicle, and a means to generate electricity, be aware that modern electric vehicles contain a remote kill switch in the batteries. If a customer does not maintain their monthly battery rental fees the vehicle will be remotely disabled. This may have occurred with any electrical vehicle you find.

As a last resort, you may need to use bicycles and other people-powered methods of transport. The most important consideration with any vehicle is stealth. You should be as silent and unseen as possible.

If you are travelling at night, either in a vehicle or on foot, you should avoid using lights if at all possible as these lights will open you wide up to attack. If you need to use a light make sure it is red and set to the lowest possible brightness. A red light will be more difficult to notice at a distance and will not be bright enough to completely destroy your own night vision. If you can, try to get your hands on a good quality set of night vision goggles.

If you are a pilot, whether private or commercial you may think that the aviation infrastructure will collapse during the zombie apocalypse but this is not the case. If you are a commercial pilot who flies an aircraft of 737 size or bigger, and you possess a conscience and have moral values on human life, you should move from your home in the early days of the apocalypse as military personnel will drag you from your home and force you to fly. You will be told that you are flying survivors to their safety but this will be a lie. You will be flying full plane loads to their certain death and your own survival will not be guaranteed.

Fuel

Most petroleum fuels, petrol, diesel, etc. contain preservatives that will break down after 1 year. This means that you will only have the use of petroleum based vehicles for only 1 year. If you have a vehicle and a source of fuel then make the most of this during the first year of the zombie apocalypse. It will become difficult to get petrol as the fuel pumps at petrol stations will no longer function. You will need to keep an eye out for alternative fuel sources during this first year. You might be able to secure some solar panels or a wind generator that can be used to power an electric vehicle. Some preppers have been successful in converting a petroleum based engine to run on steam, with a wood burning steam generator attached to the back of the vehicle. This would take a lot of mechanical knowledge and ingenuity to perfect.

Navigation

In today's society, we are used to navigating by GPS, either inbuilt or through our smartphones. We can easily travel without a map by following road signs. During the zombie apocalypse, most road signs will be removed, either by the military or by people looking for metal sheets, maybe for building defences.

GPS systems are reliant on signals sent from satellites. These satellites are synchronised by atomic clocks here on Earth. These atomic clocks must be updated daily in order to keep the whole system synchronised. Even if you have electrical power, GPS systems will become worthless in a very short time.

When travelling always bring a working compass and ordinance survey map of your surroundings. If you are travelling a short distance during the day make sure to leave for your house as early as possible in case you become trapped or your vehicle fails and you need to continue on foot. If at all possible, try to be under cover by nightfall.

In the early days create a compass calibration area at your house. To do this, place your compass on the floor and, using a permanent marker, place marks at the North, South, East and West points. Anytime you are leaving the house place your compass in the centre of these marks and make sure that your compass corresponds correctly with these markings.

Tools

If you live in a big city than the biggest tools you may have used in the past are maybe a screwdriver, electric drill and a hammer. Things are generally very easy to fix because you can always call a plumber, carpenter, electrician, etc. but those days will end once the zombie apocalypse begins. You will not only need to learn how to use tools but you will also need to do looting raids in order to gather the required tools.

Let's say that it is 6 months after the beginning of the apocalypse and you have established a permanent house. In the shed or outhouse, you might find some standard tools plus a bunch of powerful electric tools. Unless you have the ability to produce electric power than you might as well throw out those electric power tools as they will be worthless to you. Even if you are able to produce electricity the batteries on these tools require a considerable amount of power to fully charge and standard plug-in electric tools consume an incredible amount of power in comparison to the amount of electricity you may be able to produce.

If you do have a power generation system, solar or wind power, it will be best if you charge power tool batteries rather than plugging in corded power tools as these will consume all of your electrical power reserves in a very short time. The best scenario is to wait until you need to do a lot of work with power tools. Have an efficient plan for when the batteries are fully charged and use the tool sparingly.

Some non-power tools that can be useful include:

- Screwdriver with replaceable head
- Screwdriver heads (various types / sizes)
- Clawhammer
- Pliers (various sizes)
- Adjustable wrench
- Tape measure
- Spirit level
- Box cutter
- Hacksaw
- Stud finder
- Socket wrench

- Allen keys (various sizes)
- Crosscut saw
- Chisels (various sizes)
- Shovel
- Wheelbarrow
- Step ladder
- Clamps
- Sledgehammer
- Vice grip pliers
- Snow shovel (depending on where you live)
- Craft knives (extremely sharp knives)
- Plumbing tape
- Duct tape
- Glue
- Hand operated drill
- Drill bits (various sizes)

Gather as many tools as possible. You never know what kind of tool you may need or when you may need it. The ability to drive down to the local hardware store will be gone. Any time you are using tools or doing any hardware work it is vital to maintain as much silence as possible. Even if you think the area is clear of any dangers you never know who or what can hear you. Sound travels very far.

If you are useless with tools and general DIY I suggest that you learn from any friends who have tools and know how to use them. If you ever have workmen in your house or apartment learn as much as you can from them. Don't get in their way but do watch them carefully so you can learn what to do.

Further Disasters

Just because the world has fallen foul to a zombie apocalypse does not mean that natural disasters have stopped. These natural disasters will continue to strike the Earth long after humans are gone.

Drought

Drought is caused when there are long periods of sunny weather and an extreme lack of rainfall. You may need to ration what water supplies you have as any wells you have built could quickly dry up and streams could evaporate to a trickle very quickly.

When drought sets in it is important to conserve as much water as possible. Avoid washing in order to save water for drinking. If you use any water for anything other than drinking be sure to reuse that water for other things such as washing clothes rather than throwing it away.

If the drought persists for more than 6 months it may be better to abandon your house and travel to cooler climates. Depending on where you are in relation to the equator this will either be North or South. If you come across a coastline **do not** get tempted to drink sea water as this will kill you. At some stage, you will more than likely come across a fresh water stream.

Forest fire

During dry summer months, large uncontrollable forest fires can be sparked by lightning. Wheat fields have been known to spontaneously burst into flames without any obvious ignition source when they become bone dry and the weather is unbelievably hot. Forest fires are driven by high winds and in most cases, they will prove to be impossible to outrun in some areas.

If you live near a forest or wooded area and see a fire in the distance be prepared to evacuate. As these fires can travel very fast it is best to leave your house long before it reaches you. Leave the wooded area and keep yourself out in the open. Monitor the fire from a distance to ensure it is not coming in your direction.

If you do need to escape through the fire cover yourself with a wet blanket and run as fast as you can. Do not stop while in the fire and when you finally get out the other side check to see if you are on fire. If you are you must immediately drop to the ground and roll around until the flames are extinguished.

Nuclear attack

A nuclear war will most likely **not** break out during a zombie apocalypse as each country will be facing an internal situation rather than nations facing off against other nations. However, as the zombie apocalypse spreads uncontrollably most soldiers in nuclear missile commands will either be killed or go on the run in order to save themselves or their families. Nuclear weapon systems require constant maintenance and will ultimately degrade and suffer over time.

In 1983 a nuclear early warning system in Russia malfunctioned and showed that America had launched some intercontinental ballistic missiles. The Russian officer in command quickly realised that the system was incorrect and the report must be false. This happened twice that day and on both occasions, the Russian officer in command put a stop to the alarms. Had he not reacted the Russian system would have launched its missiles against America and would have resulted in a worldwide nuclear war. The officer in command who is responsible for averting nuclear war on that day was Stanislav Yevgrafovich Petrov.

In a post-apocalyptic world, a nuclear war will not be triggered by humans but will most likely be triggered by the machines that run the system. These computer systems will degrade, detect a false alarm and launch a single missile. This single missile will trigger more and more nukes to launch. The result will be worldwide thermo-nuclear war. While the single world government will try their best to prevent this from happening it is inevitable that accidental nuclear war will occur. This event may happen 5 years, 10 years or 20 years after the beginning of the apocalypse.

The first thing you must survive is the explosive blast and the heat wave. If you see a super bright light suddenly appear you **must not** look at this light or you will go instantly blind. You may only have seconds to react. Dive for the nearest available cover, a bunker, a natural dip in the ground or any form of shelter that is at or below ground level. Cover all exposed skin immediately as this will suffer extreme burns once the heat wave hits.

When the blast wave expands it will generate very strong pressures that will destroy buildings and anything else in its way. This will cause millions of objects to fly over your head and all around you at very high speeds. Once the blast has passed you, do not become complacent as there is more to come. A vacuum will be created by the initial blast and air will rush back to the point of the blast, to fill this vacuum, at high speeds. This will result in further damage and devastation. After this the heat wave will follow, burning everything in its wake.

If you survive the initial blast and heat wave you will be faced with radioactive fallout. This will slowly fall to the ground approximately 20-30 minutes after the blast and will render water undrinkable and earth unusable for growing food. If you are lucky you will have a fully stocked and equipped bunker to hide in. If you are unlucky you will now need to survive a radiated Earth as well as everything else you are facing on a daily basis.

A Geiger counter will be vital for future survival at this point. You must use this Geiger counter for checking radiation levels in any food or water that you will be consuming.

Zombie migrations

As time goes on and as food becomes more scarce zombies may gather in large groups. These groups may migrate across whole countries devouring everything in sight, similar to locusts. These groups of zombies spell certain death to anyone in their path. If you are able to view such a migration from a distance it will afford you some valuable minutes to gather your supplies and run.

Although the zombies in these migrations will not be running at full speed, they will at least be walking pretty fast. Do not waste any time in getting as far away from these migrations as possible. Staying where you are and trying to defend your house will almost guarantee certain death. As with thieves today, you cannot stop a zombie from getting into your house, you can only slow him down. If anyone is determined to get in they will, and zombies will not give up like a human might. Do not engage these large migrations in battle. You will lose. Do not join any form of resistant movement that will attack one of these migrations. They will lose.

Tsunami

As we have seen from the Indian Ocean tsunami of 2004 and the Japan tsunami of 2011, this kind of disaster can cause mass destruction and loss of life within a very short period of time. Tsunamis can be triggered by undersea earthquakes as well as massive landslides. You may not feel any earthquake but still be hit by a tsunami that originates thousands of kilometres away.

During the zombie apocalypse, any early warning systems will no longer be working or will no longer be monitored. You will need to watch for signs yourself. If you are at a coastline and notice any unusual fluctuations in sea level, such as a dramatic rise or fall, this is a sign that a tsunami may be approaching. Another indicator is a very loud roaring sound coming from far out in the ocean.

Tsunamis come in multiple waves. The first wave will not be the largest one so if you see a sudden large wave wash ashore farther than normal it could be an indication that a tsunami is imminent.

If you do see any warning signs take action immediately by going to the highest ground possible. Do not return to your home to gather supplies as a tsunami will travel very fast and you may become trapped in your house. You can pre-arrange a cache of emergency supplies to be hidden on a high point close to your home in case you are faced with such a disaster. During a tsunami, the waves will continually come inland and retreat only to repeat this process over and over for several hours. The water could take several days to fully recede.

Flood

Floods can occur at any time and will generally be more devastating in low-lying areas. Pay close attention to where your house is located. Are you in a valley? Is there a dam anywhere close to your house? Dams require constant monitoring and maintenance and without this are at risk of eventually collapsing. If this happens a torrent of water may sweep through your neighbourhood causing mass devastation.

Rainfall can cause flooding in your neighbourhood or could even cause too much ground water at a location far from your house but this could travel, ultimately settling in your area. If you notice that water is rapidly rising it is best if you stay in your house and retreat to the upper floors.

High-rise buildings provide some of the best protection because you can keep going up floor after floor until the flood stops.

When you see floodwater forming it is time to gather food and fresh drinking water. You will not be able to rely on the floodwater itself for drinking as this will be highly contaminated with chemicals and dead animals or people.

Some floods can overwhelm two-story houses. In this case, **do not** evacuate to the attic as you may become trapped there. Instead, when the flood waters are still low, get to the attic and prepare to smash a hole through the roof. Return to the lower floors and carefully monitor the flood water. Should the level reach halfway up the stairs go to the attic and smash through the roof. Take a break every 2 minutes to re-check the water level. If the level is up to the second floor do not return to the attic to finish the job. Instead, evacuate through an upstairs window, into the flood water and hold on for dear life.

Tornado

If you live in an area that is prone to tornados you will need to move to a more hospitable region as soon as possible. You may have been used to having your house blown away every year, only for it to be rebuilt by the insurance company, but those days are long gone. If your house is blown away you will be simply left without a house and with no possible way to replace it. All of your supplies will be blown away also. How long did it take you to gather those supplies?

Living in an area that is not prone to tornadoes will still not be a guarantee that one will not develop and sweep through your region. You will most likely hear a tornado coming before you see it. If at all possible it is best to evade a tornado rather than staying in your house. This carries its own risks as debris can travel at tremendous speeds and cars can be blown away as if they were toy cars.

If a tornado makes a direct hit on your house it will completely destroy it and suck all objects into the air. If you are one of the things sucked up into the air you stand little to no chance of survival. If you know a tornado is in the area take shelter in the basement of your house. If your house does not have a basement area go to the centre of the ground floor. Always stay clear of the windows as these can easily explode causing severe injuries. If you have a downstairs bathroom climb into the bath, as this is usually a very heavy item that may stay put while the rest of your house gets blown away.

Once a tornado has passed, check the structure of your house, if it has survived, to make sure that all structural walls are in good condition. Make sure that all defensive walls around your house are stable and free from large cracks.

Earthquake

If you live in an earthquake-prone region of Earth, or you live near a fault line, whether it is active or not, then the possibility exists that you will at some stage need to survive an earthquake. Any early warning systems that you may be used to will be long gone and you may not receive any advanced warning of an impending earthquake as a result. Animals can give an indication but these warnings may only come seconds before a quake. If your dog, cat or other domestic pet suddenly jumps up and runs in a panic it could be an indication or instabilities in the crust of the Earth that could warn of a possible earthquake. The chances are that this warning will be so short that you will still be wondering what's up with your pet when the quake happens.

When an earthquake hits it is best if you can immediately run outside to a wide open area that does not contain any trees, electrical pylons or anything else that can fall on you. If this is not possible then get under a sturdy table or under a door frame. If possible extinguish any fires you may have lighting as these could be scattered and cause your house to catch fire. Wait until the tremor has stopped.

Be aware that many aftershocks may follow. You will need to check your house to see if it is structurally sound. If your house is not structurally sound it is safer to abandon your house and never return.

Expect all structures in the region to be compromised by the earthquake and keep this in mind when finding a new house to live in.

Gas mains, although out of commission for many years, may still contain gas. During an earthquake, these pipes may be ruptured spreading dangerous amounts of concentrated gases into the area. Sniff around your house after an earthquake and if you smell gas immediately gather your supplies and leave as soon as possible.

Supervolcano

This one ranks as high as a worldwide thermonuclear war in its destructive ability. There are approximately 6 supervolcanoes on Earth with the most likely one to erupt being the Yellowstone Caldera in Wyoming USA. Should this super volcano erupt it is likely to cause a single, yet gigantic, eruption that will last about one week. Unlike a regular volcano that will spew lava over an extensive time period, this super volcano will expel massive quantities of lava into the air in a week long powerful explosion. This lava will cool down and fall to the ground as a gooey hot rock but will be limited to about 65 km (40 miles) around the Yellowstone national park area.

The most damaging aspect of a supervolcano erupting is the ash cloud generated by the blast that will linger in the upper atmosphere for several years. This will block out enough sunlight to affect vegetation growth worldwide. You will need a stock of food that is capable of lasting upwards of 4 years if you are to stand a chance of surviving a super volcano eruption. If you rely on solar panels to supply your house with electrical power this will be badly hindered by the ash cloud and may reduce the power generating capacity to either a trickle of power or nothing at all.

How Long Could It Last

Expect the zombie apocalypse to last for the rest of your life. Even if the zombies are killed off or starve to death you will still remain at danger from other humans and the military. The latter will become the most dangerous, more dangerous than even the zombies themselves. Expect zombies to roam the Earth for up to 2 years following the beginning of this viral attack. The worst period will be within the first 6 months when chaos will reign supreme.

In the first 6 months, you will see vast amounts of people being killed by zombies, a general lack of compassion from other living people (due to fear and panic) and great amounts of people choosing suicide rather than trying to continue attempting to survive. This short period of time will see the worst aspects of humanity coming to the surface.

Within the first year, you will see military forces sweeping through cities and taking truckloads of civilians away. Many zombies will continue to roam and some humans will be left behind. Not everyone will be taken. **Do not go with the military**.

About 2 years after the beginning of the zombie apocalypse you will notice that you rarely encounter a zombie. Their numbers have dwindled significantly and the end of the zombie era is close. Drones will begin to slowly dominate the sky. You must avoid these drones at all costs.

Within 5 years you may notice that new cities or superhighways are being built. You may hear the construction or see it with your own eyes. Do not get a false sense of safety. Do not approach the worksites and do not attempt to volunteer to help. The people building these cities will not live very long, do not join their ranks.

Within 10 years the world population will have been stripped of over 80% of its previous levels. New, fantastic looking cities will exist and you may encounter defectors who have left the cities. They will tell you stories of how fantastically they live in these cities yet they are still defecting from these areas. You are better off staying where you

are if you have managed to survive for this
long.

Possible Timeline of Events

Day 1
- Chaos reigns supreme
- Mass killings by zombies
- Looting begins

Day 2
- Chaos reigns supreme
- Looting continues
- Mass shootings by police forces

Day 3
- Chaos reigns supreme
- Looting continues
- Military now on city streets

Week 1

- Chaos reigns supreme
- Marshal law enacted worldwide
- Going into the street will get you shot

Month 1

- Chaos reigns supreme
- Suicides begin
- Military sweeps begin

Month 3

- Chaos reigns supreme
- Suicides continue
- Military sweeps continue

Month 6

- Chaos reigns supreme
- Suicides reach their peak
- Military sweeps continue

Year 1
- Military sweeps should stop soon
- Drone sweeps begin
- Trading for supplies becomes more acceptable

Year 3
- No more zombies roaming the Earth
- Drone sweeps continue
- Consider removing or marking the location of all booby traps

Year 5
- Drone sweeps continue
- Massive construction of superhighways and new cities begins
- Human population level reduced to approximately 1 billion
- Machine triggered thermonuclear war

Year 10
- Drone sweeps dwindle dramatically
- City defections begin

Year 15

- City defections continue
- World population now less than 500 million

Year 20

- Social system in the new cities break down completely
- Massive deaths in the cities due to starvation

Conclusion

The zombie apocalypse is survivable and I hope that you are one of those people who will, not only survive, but thrive. You may spend time gathering supplies only for them to be taken from you or you may fall victim to the zombie virus but don't let any of this stop you because it hasn't happened yet.

If you do fall victim to the zombie virus it will happen within the first 3 months. After this time, if you are free from infection you will either survive, be enslaved, or die. Being enslaved will ultimately result in your death so you better survive.

Survival is more about having a survivalist mindset rather than having countless supplies and weapons. Throughout the entire history of human beings, it is clear to see that we are designed to survive. We can acclimatise ourselves to almost any conditions no matter how severe. Most fish will die within hours if their environment suffers temperature fluctuations of only a few degrees yet we can survive in the coldest or hottest of climates. As cavemen, we managed to survive on limited supplies and during very dangerous times.

You are a survivor whether you know it or not. There are people on this planet who are determined to wipe out over 80% of us. You do not need to rely on them for your survival. You can live through this and things will even become comfortable after only a few years. Those years will fly by as you busy yourself building defences, gathering supplies and fighting off your enemies.

I wish you continued survival during the coming zombie apocalypse.

About Tadhg O'Flaherty

As a computer whizz-kid, Tadhg was naturally inept at writing until he discovered that by utilising the Law of Attraction he was able to seamlessly transition into the field and is now a full-time author with several books currently self-published on Amazon.

Tadhg's second book "Surviving a Realistic Zombie Apocalypse" gained local notoriety within days of publishing and was featured on the front page of the Limerick Leader newspaper, which has a readership of 110,290 and also received airtime on local and national radio.

To find out more, visit Tadhg's website and sign up to the author's mailing list for advanced notice of new releases, promotions and more.

www.tadhgfla.com

Author's Note

Thank you for reading **Surviving a Realistic Zombie Apocalypse**. I hope you enjoyed this book. Word-of-mouth is vital for the success of any author. Please consider leaving a review on Amazon. Each review makes all the difference and would be greatly appreciated.

Also by Tadhg O'Flaherty

How to Get Over Her in 1 Month: Learn how to rise like a Phoenix from the ashes of a breakup

Prepper's: The Ultimate Guide

Living Off-Grid

Living a Happy Life

Living a Productive Life

Do You Really Exist?

How to Reprogram Your Subconscious

Surviving Crippling Poverty